Published in 1998 and distributed in the U.S. by
Stewart, Tabori & Chang,
a division of U.S. Media Holdings, Inc.
115 West 18th Street, New York, NY 10011

Distributed in Canada by
General Publishing Company Ltd.
30 Lesmill Road
Don Mills, Ontario, M3B 2T6, Canada

Distributed in all other territories by
Grantham Book Services Ltd.
Isaac Newton Way, Alma Park Industrial Estate
Grantham, Lincolnshire, NG31 9SD England

ISBN: 1-55670-735-5

Library of Congress Catalog Card Number: 97-62056

Printed in Belgium
10 9 8 7 6 5 4 3 2 1

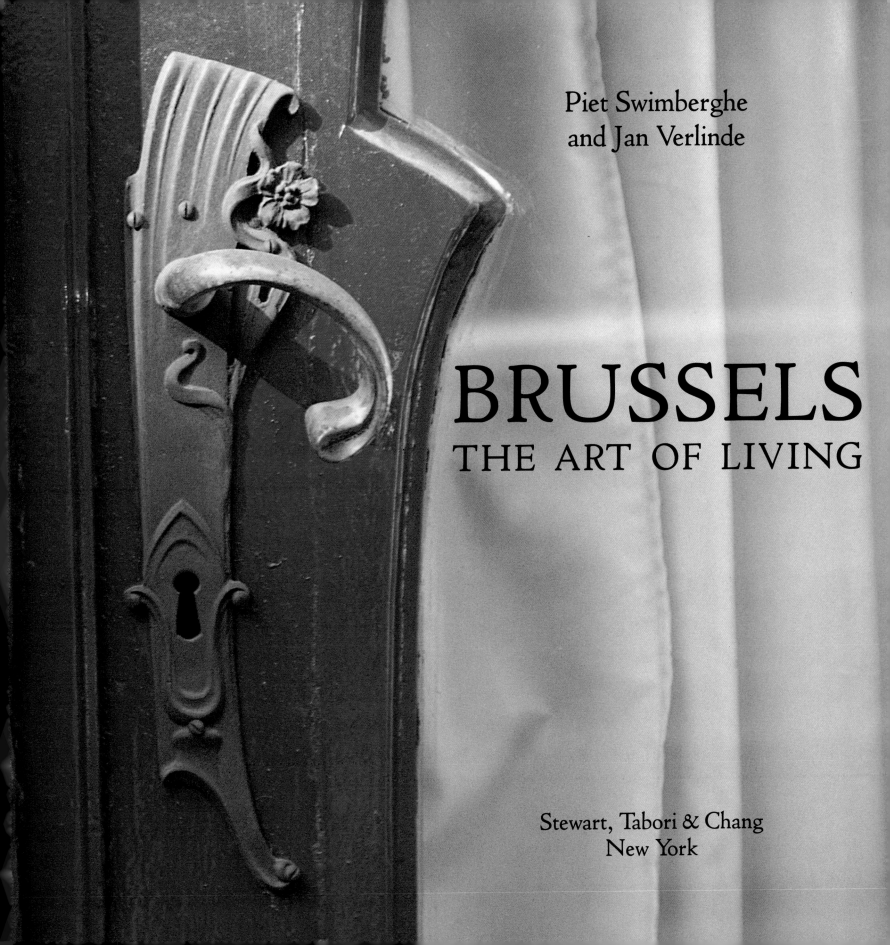

Piet Swimberghe
and Jan Verlinde

BRUSSELS
THE ART OF LIVING

Stewart, Tabori & Chang
New York

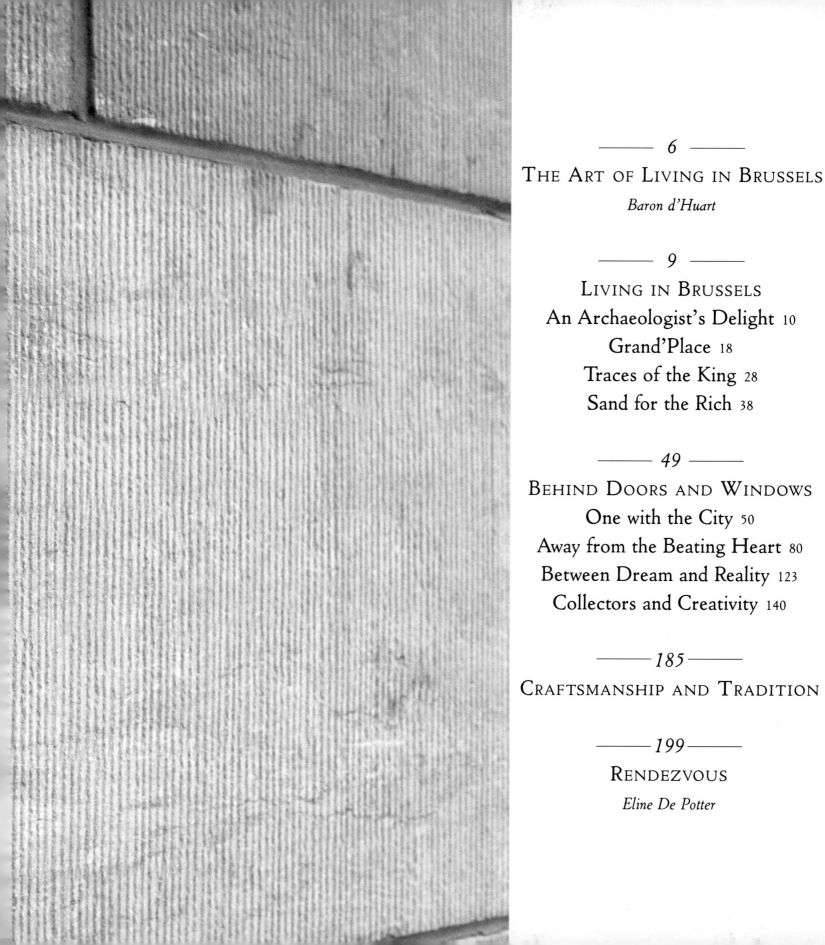

The Art
of Living
in Brussels

Life in Brussels is full of surprises. This city, which is much nearer to you than you may think, has many unexpected discoveries in store. Brussels may overwhelm you at first with its many places of interest, and this may prevent you from thoroughly enjoying this multi-faceted city right from the start. Thus a concise guide like this entertaining and instructive book will prove useful. So read on.

Capital of a duchy, capital of a kingdom, capital of a continent, Brussels is much more than what can be gleaned from the histories of Brabant, Belgium and Europe.

The city's historical splendour as described in beautiful gilt lettering in leather-bound books takes us back to the feudal times of proud knights and noble ladies – and yet, the history of Brussels has been one of a perpetual struggle for financial dominance between its rulers and its several municipalities.

Brussels is a bourgeois, rather than a feudal city. Its dignitaries and burghers have always been keen businessmen. The real key to Brussels is to be found in this down-to-earth business sense.

From the Gothic era the people of Brussels have inherited a deep distrust of empty spaces. Gothic architecture was worked like coral and sculpted like a piece of art – every single detail was finished to perfection. The people of Brussels never felt comfortable with things that have no practical use.

A few popular wisdoms that have survived from the Renaissance – 'everything in moderation' and 'mankind is the measure of all things' – sum up the essence of Brussels philosophy and art. Many things may still be beyond the ken of man, but this does not stop us from admiring subtle details and trying to perpetuate these in works of art that are invariably practical and colourful. The Brussels tapestries from the past testify both to the delight felt by painters and weavers when they glimpsed a dewdrop on a flower, a snail on a twig, a frog in a moor or a bird in the air, and to their keen sense of usefulness in beauty, propriety in amusement and sophistication in genius.

During the Baroque era the spirit of Rubens enhanced realism, elevating it to a more lofty dimension. Even major allegorical works invariably contained some mundane detail, such as a waffle at the Banquet of the Gods. But details like these were made to transcend mere reality, as indicated by a still life of fishes shaped like jewels. The people of Brussels were enterprising, down-to-earth merchants, prosperous and modest, reliable and friendly. In this they differed very much, indeed, from the Florentines, always on the lookout for thought-provoking, exclusive novelties, from the Venetians, permanently engaged in the search for Byzantium, incense and velvet, from the Parisians, never content with anything less than magnificent elegance, and from the Londoners, obsessed by rural landscapes, undulating like the sea...

I am convinced that no-one born and bred in Brussels will have read the preceding sentence to the end; the people of Brussels tend to lose interest once they become aware that the story is not about them, so they will start leafing the pages of this beautiful book to see if more is said about them elsewhere. The next paragraph will excite their interest again.

The people of Brussels have never allowed themselves to sink into insignificance. When French troops destroyed Grand'Place at the end of the seventeenth century, the exhausted inhabitants hastened to rebuild it, dressing the yawning Gothic wounds with gilt Baroque ornamentation. When Napoleon pulled down the city fortifications the people of Brussels responded by planting a forest along the newly created wide avenues. When Mont des Arts was dug up to make place for new streets, King Leopold II proposed to pay for everything out of his own pocket, so impatient was he to see what the new part of the city would look like. He had fountains built and flowerbeds laid out. Young couples in love would saunter along the new streets, artists would come for a stroll, dreaming of Progress. But the greatest transformation of all was still to come... The World Fair of 1958 brought about an architectural catastrophe that has done irreparable harm to Brussels. The city was torn apart, its bowels and heart exposed, its inhabitants driven out, its squares and suburbs razed. This frenzy of construction continued for as long as the flirt between Brussels and Progress lasted. The 1958 World Fair was a triumph, but like so many triumphs it ended in disaster. Its only lasting achievement is a wide strip of concrete covering the destroyed parts of the city. But I still feel the need to tell of my experiences in these lost parts of the city.

When I say 'my experiences', what I mean is 'their experiences'. The experiences of my friends, my family, my loved ones. Brussels was home to them, and to me. Brussels, with its Quartier Leopold, one of the last strongholds of the aristocracy flaunting its grand avenues and magnificent mansions to the east of the Royal Palace. Servants, horses and trees were plentiful, and there was a good deal of informal familiarity. Everyone was family. Friendship was the keyword. The local grocer would address the countess of [...] in a most familiar fashion, without anyone knowing the reason why. In fact, it only enhanced the countess's prestige. The milkman delivered milk in Rue Belliard. The money to pay for the milk would be left under a brick or a tile. People still trusted their neighbours.

Sablon, south of Place Royale, used to be a neighbourhood where princes intermingled with the poor in perfect harmony. The antique dealers had not yet moved in, but even then the neighbourhood could boast of many notable antiques. The Prince of Arenberg's collection in Egmont Palace was definitely worth a visit, and the garden of his neighbour, the Count of Mérode, was so huge that it became the site of the Palais de Justice, whose Babylonian design makes it one of the nineteenth-century's most colossal buildings.

But all this showiness did not at all intimidate the people of the Marolles, the district below Sablon. Many colourful anecdotes, and some regrettable ones as well, are told about the Marolles: it is said that when Ursel Palace was demolished, its owner, a countess, simply sent for a local second-hand dealer, who carried off whole cartloads of period furniture that had become 'superfluous'.

Isn't that a typical example of the art of living? In fact, hasn't the art of living become superfluous as well? Hasn't it become a relic of the past, much like old palaces and lace doilies put under empty vases? Brussels has developed its own particular mode of survival, which consists of reclaiming the best from man-made disasters, and of turning inhuman tragedies into something bearable. Most people now think of Brussels as an unusually agreeable place to live in, despite its ugliness.

The following pages will enable you to test the truth of this opinion. The beautiful exteriors and often subdued interiors shown there have at least one thing in common: they were designed with love.

Love in its Brussels variety – efficient, realistic, without any concessions to dishonesty, ugliness, imitativeness or kitsch and wholly devoted to making the art of living more enjoyable.

You have been warned.   Baron d'Huart

Living in Brussels

From Gare du Midi to the European Quarter is less than thirty minutes on foot. During this short walk we will encounter an enormous variety of cultures and architectural styles. Brussels is not a large city, but it has countless faces – around every street corner a different neighbourhood beckons, either reminding us of the past or making us glimpse the future.

An Archaeologist's Delight

Whether you come to Brussels through the Pajottenland, between the Dendre and the Senne, or along the rim of the forest of Soignes through Linkebeek and Tervuren and eventually to Brussels, everywhere you turn you will see Bruegelian landscapes with rutted roads and gently undulating hills. Nowadays, of course, you have to leave the motorway and look beyond the dreary housing developments. Much of this landscape, unfortunately, has virtually disappeared. Here and there you may chance upon a chink of scenery that is intact and where in summer it is pleasant to linger a while in the shade of an oak or linden tree. It is difficult to imagine now that the city itself took root in such fertile green pastures, because the stream around which the original settlement was formed is now buried under several layers of concrete. However, anyone who searches with determination will find subtle reminders of an illustrious past in the names of houses, streets and squares. As you stroll round Brussels you have to have the patience of an archaeologist to tease out the history of this city because many vestiges of the past have disappeared.

WHENEVER I SET OUT TO EXPLORE Brussels, I always bring along a pair of rubber boots and a small trowel. These archaeological tools prove to be highly useful for covert digs on deserted building lots, where I go to find traces of the Brussels of the past. So far, all I have discovered are crumbling old walls and a few medieval pot-shards. Most parts of Brussels have quite literally been turned upside down by bulldozers and shovel-wielding labourers in an attempt to destroy the past. More than other cities, Brussels seems to have got rid of its history. The little that remains can only be discovered by studying the city's current layout from an archeological perspective. Ever since the mid-nineteenth century Brussels has been growing at a tremendous rate. Just a few generations ago suburbs like Schaerbeek and Ixelles were still rural villages. The River Senne, flowing through the heart of Brussels, was tunnelled in and hidden below new houses and streets. Picturesque working-class neighbourhoods were demolished to make room for wide boulevards reminiscent of Paris. An underground railway was built to connect the Gare du Nord and the Gare du Midi. In recent times vast quantities of concrete were used to build the many office blocks that have emerged along this underground route.

Even so, some traces of Brussels' earliest origins can still be found. Though not very spectacular, they hold a certain interest. During my explorations of building lots I have often noticed that the subsoil is unusually damp. The reason is that the oldest parts of Brussels were built on marshy soil. These marshes were interrupted by low, undulating hills and cut through by meandering brooks in a Bruegelian decor. Agriculture flourished in the fertile fields, where a rich variety of vegetables were grown. The many woods and forests contained an abundance of game. The area was a culinary paradise and generously provided the ingredients for a truly epicurean cuisine. Today, only the names of a few streets remind us of those bygone days. One of them is Rue de la Grande Ile (Great Island Street), connecting Place St Géry and Place Fontainas. This street, originally an island in the River Senne, is supposed to have been the site of the stronghold around which the city developed a thousand years ago. Virtually nothing from this period has remained, not even the thirteen watermills that once graced the inner city. A tiny part of the Senne can still be seen behind the *Gulden Leeuw*, an old house on a corner of Place St Géry. Unfortunately, this area was restored in the worst of taste.

A stone's throw away a small harbour was built, enclosed by Rue Ste Catherine, Rue de la Vierge Noire and Rue de l'Evêque. Despite its limited size – not to be compared with major ports like Ghent or Bruges – it contributed to the further development of Brussels. In its immediate vicinity a marketplace was laid out, lined by large new houses. But it would be many centuries yet before Grand'Place acquired its current appearance. In the early Middle Ages Brussels was still a provincial backwater. It took quite a long time for the town to grow. The Senne played no part in the development of Brussels. The town owed its growth to its location on the Bruges to Cologne trade route. This was one of the major arteries of Western Europe, particularly from the 12th century onwards. At that time improved harnesses helped to drive out oxen as draught-animals in favour of horses. Another innovation was the introduction of four-wheeled carts to replace two-wheeled ones, shortening journeys and leading to more rapid transport. Along the trade route towns that were a single day's

journey apart began to flourish. Merchants would travel from Ghent to Alost and Brussels and continue from there to Leuven, Tienen, Zoutleeuw, Maastricht and Cologne. Brussels owed its prosperity to the horse. In the 13th century it even began to rival Leuven.

Miraculously, Brussels has preserved a few souvenirs from its youth. They can be found in the northern part of the city, where most of today's slums are concentrated. You won't meet many tourists in this thinly populated and impoverished area. But from an archeological viewpoint it is probably the most interesting part of Brussels. It was here that the soul of Brussels was shaped by craftsmen and merchants. Finding the few relics of the past is quite a challenge. Most visitors to the city make straight for Grand'Place or for Coudenberg with their imposing historical monuments. These were the rich man's parts of Brussels; they are not the proletarian Brussels that inspired Bruegel.

It is in the north of the city that we find most of the remnants of the medieval trade route. Merchants would cross the canal at Chaussee de Gand in Molenbeek, pass through the city gate and arrive in Rue de Flandre. Anyone trying to follow in their footsteps will now take the wrong direction. The modern bridge across the canal keeps the old trade route on its left and leads to Rue Dansaert, a street built only last century. It quite overshadows narrow, winding Rue de la Comtesse de Flandre, which remains hidden to most passers-by. It is clear that no-one wants to set up shop here. The peeling façades look sadly derelict. The street is in a state of unrelieved decay, without the least hint of quaintness. And yet, in a time long past tradesmen and craftsmen earned a good living here. The price of land was so high that every square inch was put to use. Even the gardens

and passageways were used for building. Rue de la Cigogne evokes memories from those days. This dark, narrow lane has regained at least some of its charm because several houses have been restored. The entrance to the lane is guarded by Saint Rochus, the patron saint of plague sufferers; he reminds us of the time when the inhabitants of the harbour district were among the first victims of this terrible disease.

At the end of Rue de Flandre we turn back, by way of Rue du Vieux Marché aux Grains, to Grande Ile. The castle that once stood here was soon deserted by its occupants, who moved downtown to hold court on Coudenberg. But the harbour district grew in importance. Ships would unload their cargoes of cloth, which were then transported by cart to Paris. Brussels cloth – a woollen material as thick as felt – was much in demand. It was more expensive than Byzantine velvet and highly popular among the French nobility. By the end of the 14th century, however, the fashion had passed and demand fell. Brussels then switched to tapestry weaving, as did Tournai, Arras and Paris. The major weaving mills were situated on Rue du Marché au Charbon, near Grand'Place, in a traditional cloth manufacturing area. I suspect there was yet another reason why so many weaving mills were located near the financial heart of the city. Tapestries were woven for rich patrons, so the workshops had to be housed in fairly dignified buildings where prospective clients could be received in style. And not just clients, but also the money-lenders who helped to finance the mills. Large investments were required because tapestry weaving is an immensely slow process. The manufacturers turned to Italian, German and Antwerp bankers for financial support.

Five centuries ago the busiest part of Brussels was the area near Grand'Place and Eglise Ste Catherine. This confusing maze of streets and alleys,

13

The variety of styles that characterises Brussels façades knows no boundaries. There is every possible form imaginable of Art Nouveau, like the example shown here that graces avenue Victor Rousseau (left). Around the turn of the century, architects were conjuring up new forms with the most diverse building materials, from glazed bricks to tiles and iron, which was used in many different ways. One of the finest examples is undoubtedly the former Old England shop on rue Montagne de la Cour. This imposing work of art that dates from just before the turn of the century was designed by architect Paul Saintenoy. This is a transparent building whose façade was designed according to the distribution of space in the shop. In addition, the Brussels cityscape features every possible form of modernism, such as the monumental brick façade of the Wolfers house built in 1930 in rue Alphonse Renard by Henry Van de Velde.

where tall, stately buildings alternate with small, modest ones, was a meeting-ground for merchants, money-changers and craftsmen. The bustle and activity that were so typical of this part of Brussels continued unabated for several centuries and even survived World War II. But nowadays, although Grand'Place and the streets nearby are lively enough, the working-class neighbourhoods present a rather desolate aspect. The decline of the northern part of Brussels is rooted in its past. It began with the filling-in of the harbour docks. In fact, the names of the quays are the only reminder of a period when water was abundant here. The Ste Catherine dock was the first to be filled in, and by the beginning of this century all the other docks had gone as well. Gone, too, was the picturesque character of the harbour district. An early 19th-century lithograph of the Ste Catherine dock shows the elegant baroque spire of Eglise Ste Catherine with several sailing ships in the foreground. It almost reminds one of an Amsterdam townscape. Even last century, when its heyday was long past, the harbour district retained its special character. Old picture postcards portray nostalgic scenes of dockers shouldering bags and fishwives selling whelks and mussels. Fresh seafood was always available in Brussels because of the town's direct link to the Scheldt and the sea. Late 19th-century photographs show large quantities of building materials being unloaded on the quays. Merchants began to specialize in the sale of roof tiles, bricks, mortar, pottery, glass and tropical wood. Demand was huge, because at that time Brussels went through a period of rapid growth. The materials were loaded onto horse-drawn carts and transported to Schaerbeek, Etterbeek and Saint Giles, where new suburbs were built. More than half of all the materials used for Brussels' many Art Nouveau

buildings reached the city by way of its ancient harbour.

The harbour district developed at a time when Belgium was at the height of its prosperity. The docks were dug in the middle of the 16th century. Brussels flourished like never before, but trade was hampered by transport problems. The Senne, with its many twists and bends, was silting up and difficult to navigate. In addition, the city of Mechelen charged heavy tolls on goods from Brussels. To circumvent these problems a canal was dug to link Brussels with the River Rupel, thus establishing a direct link with the Scheldt and with Antwerp. The canal was finished in 1561 and shortly afterwards most of the docks were dug. But the political troubles of the late 16th century intervened, and it took many years before Brussels could finally benefit from its harbour. The harbour district really came into its own at the time of the Twelve Years' Truce (1609-1621) during the war against the Spaniards. Old, narrow façades and dilapidated Baroque gates still testify to the former grandeur of Quai aux Briques, Quai aux Bois à Brûler and Quai du Bois de Construction. On Place Ste Catherine a handful of old buildings still rise up in their original splendour, even though they need some restoration work. The Maison de la Bellone is a fine example of the beauties of the past. This magnificent Baroque building can be reached through a covered archway on Rue de Flandre. It dates from 1697 and is crowned by the war goddess Bellona. It is now a museum and a library.

In the early 19th century the harbour district was given a new lease of life. Via the canal to Charleroi riches from Wallonia arrived. Then, unexpectedly, the railways became a major source of competition. Yet the district remained busy and lively, even after the docks had been filled in, as evidenced by the

many warehouses and half-forgotten manufactories, which are now being bought up by artists and art gallery owners. But unlike the Zuid in Antwerp it will never be a truly artistic centre. Yet something is breeding. The large number of exciting interiors proves it. Anyone going to live in this district feels the appeal of its special and multi-faceted atmosphere. Rue Dansaert shows some signs of prosperity. It has restaurants and avant-garde fashion and design shops.

During the interbellum a modern part of Brussels was built on the site of the former customs house. New buildings were constructed in the vicinity of Place de l'Yser. The first were the America Halls, built in 1925 on Boulevard de Dixmude. Luxury apartment blocks were built, *le saillant de l'Yser*, in typical French Art Deco style. The reason for all this urgent construction work was evident. This was the access route to the 1935 World Fair in Heysel Park. So all the old edifices had to go to be replaced by new construction. By now the buildings show the ravages of time. But the quadrangle of Boulevard d'Ypres and Boulevard de Dixmude is still animated. The trading traditions of the former harbour district live on in the many wholesale fruit and vegetable firms. Poverty and prosperity meet here, for just around the corner, in the Klein Kasteeltje, many refugees have found temporary shelter.

The Brussels suburb of Saint Giles is not only a pleasant place, but it is rich in beautiful townhouses. The most striking example is rue Vanderschrick, where the façades are like one enormous sculpture graced with artistically curled wrought iron. This street, designed by Ernest Blérot, was built between 1900 and 1903. Blérot gave all the houses, which are very narrow and tall, an appearance of their own by placing balconies and wooden bays everywhere, using wrought iron and a wide variety of window shapes. In this street, you will not find two front doors or letter boxes that are the same.

16

Grand'Place

IT IS RATHER FORTUNATE, I FEEL, THAT ENGI-
neers and surveyors are modern inventions, for
had they existed in the past, there can be no
doubt that Brussels would have had to do without its
famous Grand'Place. The imposing buildings encir-
cling the market square rest on marshy soil and
therefore required exceptionally strong foundations.
Wild birds like the reed-warbler used to inhabit this
region long before the town hall was built. Half of
Grand'Place is set on a sandy ridge in a swamp tra-
versed by two small brooks, Smaalbeek and Spiegel-
beek, both of which were tributaries to the River
Senne. Huge amounts of stone were needed to help
make solid foundations for the buildings. Surely, all
this effort is a clear sign of the perseverance of the
emerging bourgeoisie of Brussels. The rich burghers insisted on showing off their wealth, prosperity
and power, whatever the cost, so they built towering
buildings amidst reeds and shrubs.

Nowadays urban planners and surveyors would
immediately direct them to more appropriate areas.
Fortunately, such people were not known yet in
the Middle Ages, so Brussels was allowed to grow
and develop among brooks and pastures. The merchants built their houses wherever they liked. Near
Grand'Place small squares evolved, where poultry,
cheese, cabbages, butter, meat, vegetables and bread
were sold. This kind of trading is now definitely a
thing of the past. Only the names of the streets still
remind us of the former bazaar-like bustle. Until the
beginning of this century daily street markets took
place on Grand'Place. Only the Sunday flower and
bird markets have survived. With the increasing de-
population of the inner city most of these trading
activities have sadly come to an end.

Unfortunately, very few buildings on Grand'Place
are still in use as private residences. It is difficult to
understand why so many houses are allowed to stand
vacant, for it must be marvellous to live on
Grand'Place. The French writer Victor Hugo, who
lived in exile in Brussels during the 1850s, was thoroughly charmed by Grand'Place. He had a set of
rooms next to the Maison du Roi and would often
gaze admiringly at the magnificent town hall straight
across from his lodgings. In his *Contemplations* he
wrote:

*Tout ce qui peut tenter un coeur ambitieux
Etait là, devant moi, sur terre et dans les cieux;
Sous mes yeux, dans l'austère et gigantesque place,
J'avais les quatre points cardinaux de l'espace,
Qui fait songer a l'aigle, a l'astre, au flot, au mont,
Et les quatre pavés de l'échafaud d'Egmont.*

Hugo arrived in Brussels in 1851 and at once fell in
love with the romantic setting of Grand'Place. Nowhere in his own country could such a copiously
ornamented square be found. Even the splendid
market square of Arras pales in comparison. Hugo
understood that the fundamental difference between
the architectures of Brabant and France was not one
of styles, but of unity. French architecture followed
the dictates of the king's taste and the requirements
of the military. The French demolished entire town
centres to be able to erect elegant, but uniform buildings. From Lille to Guadeloupe all French government buildings are identical in design. French houses, too, are strikingly uniform. What Hugo admired
in Brussels was its impressive architectural variety,
where every façade differs from the rest. This virtu-
oso display is not, of course, the pinnacle of architectural achievement. But after all, that was not what it
was all about. This variety of styles reflected the
mood of a country steeped in individualism.

Grand'Place always evokes in me a feeling of
warmth that has nothing to do with beauty. No-one

can ever feel lonely here, not even in the early morning when there are no other people about. This is because the tall, narrow façades seem like a long line of human beings forming a circle around the town hall. They screen off the square from the rest of the world and protect it. History shows that the comparison is apt. When in 1421 the guilds forced the City Fathers to involve them in the administration of the city they built large guildhouses with meeting halls in Grand'Place. The members of the guilds were obstinate and self-willed craftsmen prepared to invest a lot of money in the edifices they constructed. Every single building was given a different façade to emphasise the guilds' independence from the authorities and from each other. Victor Hugo was sensitive to the charm of this piece of history, as he had had to flee from the dictatorial regime of his native country.

Even the French never succeeded in eradicating this individualism, despite all their efforts. In the summer of 1695 French troops, led by Louis XIV, burned the city. For two whole days Brussels was bombarded. There were many casualties and four thousand houses and sixteen churches were destroyed. But the aim of the French gunners was so poor that the city's most noticeable landmark, the town hall tower, escaped without a scratch. But the town hall itself was destroyed; only its walls were left standing. Two guild houses more or less survived the bombardment. But the city was very quickly rebuilt in much the same style as before, quite unlike the French style that was then fashionable. The architects and builders preferred traditional Brabant designs. The flamboyant façades are reminiscent of Rubensian Baroque, which is rooted in a more remote past. The vertical lines and the infinite decorative variety give the houses a medieval aspect. Their names, too, such as The Flying Deer, The Swan, and The Star, belong to the age of knights. The municipal authorities made a significant contribution to the rebuilding of Grand'Place. The city council wanted to harmonise the façades as much as possible. They did, indeed, create a harmonious ensemble, but complete uniformity they did not achieve. The Governor-General, Maximilian-Emmanuel of Bavaria, wanted to completely restyle Grand'Place, using uniform façades. He met with strong opposition from the people of Brussels, whose individualism made them want to emphasise their independence vis-à-vis the authorities. Only a small part of the Governor-General's design was eventually carried out. The Maison des Ducs de Brabant, set in a corner of Grand'Place, has a wide façade concealing six different houses. The entire square was to be modelled after this building. But this plan never came to fruition.

On another occasion the French once again played havoc on Grand'Place. Following the French Revolution the square was vandalised by Frenchmen who in 1793 came to remove and destroy all symbols of the *Ancien Régime*. Again, many guild houses were severely damaged. Sculpture was torn from the façades and the furniture gracing the luxurious meeting halls was burnt. The houses themselves were sold. When the guilds were finally abolished the guild houses lost their function and began to fall into disrepair. Only a few years before Victor Hugo's arrival it was proposed to demolish the entire square for the sake of progress. Just imagine! Hugo was a representative of the new mood then beginning to conquer all of Europe under the name of Romanticism. Ancient buildings begame popular again and were restored. At the end of the nineteenth century Brussels had the good fortune of having a burgomaster, Charles Buls, who was a keen amateur of history and architecture. He had many historical buildings,

Nowadays, visitors to the Galeries St Hubert would find it difficult to imagine that this fine example of architecture was erected on the site of what was a slum. In fact, on this very spot there was a narrow medieval street with tumbledown houses. According to the Dutch architect Jean-Pierre Cluysenaar, the presence of this neighbourhood close to Grand'Place was a disgrace to Brussels, the capital of the young kingdom. He therefore proposed to demolish the slum and to build in its place a prestigious arcade in the Parisian style. Eventually, after years of palaver, the first stone was laid on 6 May 1846 and the arcade was inaugurated only thirteen months later! A few years after it was opened, the arcade became the favourite haunt in wintertime of the many French exiles who had found refuge in Brussels. In the Galeries St Hubert, one came across not only writers and artists, but in the evening it was frequented by the local streetwalkers.

including those on Grand'Place, listed and restored.

Hugo was by no means the only French writer or artist to admire Grand'Place. Gérard de Nerval, Félix Tournachon, better known under his pseudonym Nadar, Théophile Gautier and even Baudelaire were also profoundly moved by its magnificent architecture. In the second half of the nineteenth century Brussels was a haven for political refugees. Many French were on the run from the tax office or had fled from Napoleon III's dictatorial regime. At the time Belgium, with its liberal Constitution and its freedom of the press, was the most democratic country in Europe. Many of the French exiles thought Brussels was a dull provincial backwater. They had a point, for Brussels only grew into a true metropolis by the end of last century. Some of the French writers said very harsh things about the city and not without reason. Many pirated editions of French novels were published in Brussels, and the novelists thus lost out on their royalties.

Many refugees would meet in the Galeries St Hubert, a shopping arcade near Grand'Place. It was the favourite meeting place of the intellectuals. Here you would encounter people like Edgar Quinet, Alexandre Dumas and the actress Juliette Drouet, Victor Hugo's mistress. She lived in rented rooms in the Galeries des Princes, branching off from Galeries St Hubert, now the site of an excellent French bookshop, *Tropismes*. Charles Baudelaire lived just round the corner, in the Hôtel du Grand Miroir, at the foot of the cathedral. In order to stay fit, he used to walk up and down the arcade eight times a day. Baudelaire, who was very scathing about Brussels, didn't really know the city very well, because he tended to stick to the same environment. On 10 July 1873 an incident happened that has gone down into the annals of literary history. On that day, the poet Paul

Verlaine bought a revolver and six cartridges from a gunshop called Montigny. He showed the gun to Arthur Rimbaud, saying, 'C'est pour toi, c'est pour moi, c'est pour tout le monde.' Then he got drunk and shot his friend.

Karl Marx was less pleased by the arcade. Driven from Paris, he settled in Brussels in 1845. It is easy to understand why he opposed the building of the arcade. It was opened in 1847, the notorious famine year. While throughout Europe vast numbers of people starved, immense wealth was displayed here. Marx could often be seen in the neighbourhood, for he and his comrade Engels held meetings of the Communist League in the Maison du Cygne on Grand'Place. A reminder of those days are the Russian and Chinese tourists who can every day be seen having their picture taken in front of the building.

It is now difficult to imagine that the Galeries St Hubert were built on the site of a former slum. A narrow medieval lane used to run here among derelict houses. The Dutch architect Jean-Pierre Cluysenaar claimed that the neighbourhood off Grand'Place was a disgrace to Brussels, the capital of a new kingdom. He suggested that the entire neighbourhood should be razed and replaced by a prestigious shopping arcade in the Paris style.

After many years of deliberations the first stone was laid on 6 May 1846. Just thirteen months later the arcade was opened! A few years later it became the favourite winter meeting-place for the many French exiles who had found refuge in Brussels. But it was not just writers and artists who frequented the arcade. At night it bcame the favourite haunt of women of easy virtue.

Galeries St Hubert is an island in the city and has hardly changed over the past hundred years. The apartments over the shops are still in use as private

Although it is not very well known to the public, lovers of old books and engravings have no difficulty in finding Galerie Bortier. This passageway, that is only a few years younger than the much more monumental Galeries St Hubert located nearby, was also designed by Cluysenaar.

residences. The old shop fronts take us back to the wealthy past. Many of the shops have a long history, such as the Ganterie Italienne, which has done business here since 1890. A bit further along there is the Taverne du Passage, a restaurant with a pure Art Deco interior. The most striking landmark in the adjacent Galerie de la Reine is a chocolate shop, Neuhaus. This is where Jean Neuhaus, a Swiss,

opened his first shop in 1857. There are also a cinema with a quaint 'forties interior, an old-fashioned theatre, bookshops, coffeeshops and fashionable clothing shops. The arcade is still a meeting-place for many residents of Brussels. Many people go here to enjoy the atmosphere and admire the architecture. The unity of design is breathtakingly beautiful. Jean-Pierre Cluysenaar, the architect, got his inspiration

from the Paris shopping arcades. This explains the truly delightful subdued Classicist design.

In the heart of the city centre there is another arcade, the Passage du Nord, linking Boulevard Adolphe Max and Rue Neuve. During the 1880s this was the most fashionable place of Brussels. It was a centre of culture with its theatres and museums that complemented the shops and restaurants.

This used to be the poshest district of the city. Some of its former splendour has been preserved in the architectural gems along the Boulevards Adolphe Max, Anspach and Maurice Lemonnier, the most beautiful avenues of Brussels. Sadly, the original harmony has been spoilt by new construction, dereliction and intrusive billboards. Worst affected is the majestic Place de Brouckère. The best thing to

This arcade leads to rue Duquesnoy. In this district you will find dozens of antique dealers offering a tremendous range of curios including Tintin comics, posters and 19th century prints. From here, you are only a stone's throw away from the antique shops of Sablon.

do is simply ignore all the decay and just admire the stately buildings. Such opulence is rare even in Paris. Today, our point of view has literally changed. Rightly so, because a tremendous amount of craftsmanship was involved in creating these splendid buildings. The interiors of the hotels, too, were superbly styled and finished. The Métropole Hotel is the most beautiful manifestation of this heyday of design and architecture. Nearby, there is the Bourse (the Stock Exchange), built like an ancient temple. Rodin lent Carrier-Belleuse a hand with the sculptures. To the left and the right of this monument to finance are the two most celebrated Brussels cafés. The Cirio is the oldest. It dates from 1886 and was famous for its Italian wines. Here the beau monde would come to enjoy a discreet glass (or two). The quiet would only be broken by the mellifluous tones of a string ensemble. The sumptuous furnishings evoked an exotic atmosphere. The furniture dates from just before Art Nouveau and is full of Renaissance motifs. On the other side of the Bourse we enter modern times. The Falstaff is pure *Belle Epoque*. It opened in 1903 and was built by Houbion, the architect and contractor. Every chair, bench, table, mirror and piece of wainscoting displays the whiplash style typical of Horta. While we enjoy a half and half, a mixture of wine and champagne, the entire decor seems to move.

If you want a taste of the Belle Epoque, why not drop into the Falstaff Tavern in the shadow of the Brussels Stock Exchange building. Art Nouveau lives again in the shimmering decor of its bright windows, cupolas and mirrors.

26

Traces
of the King

Between 1815 and 1830, when Belgium was part of the Kingdom of the Netherlands, a considerable number of striking public buildings were constructed which still grace the city skyline. Actually, the so-called Dutch period is a forgotten chapter in the history of Brussels. First of all, the Dutch built a new courthouse that was demolished in 1892. The construction of the Theatre de la Monnaie got under way in 1817. William of Orange had his own residence built next to the place where the Palace now stands. In 1824, the place des Barricades and Pacheco church were built. The Botanic Gardens (right), which are in fact a huge winter garden, were constructed between 1826 and 1829 and set the seal on the work of architects Gineste and Tilman-François Suys. This temple is surrounded by a small park with many bronze statues.

RECENTLY A HISTORIAN LOOKING THROUGH some old archives came upon a confidential letter written by King Leopold I to one of his ministers. In the letter the King stated quite unambiguously that his son was mentally disturbed. Apparently, the young prince had built a fountain complete with running water in his first-floor bedroom. His father was afraid the palace might collapse as a result. A few years later the young fountain-builder was crowned King Leopold II. During his reign – from 1865 to 1909 – he filled Brussels with scaffolding. Over a period of almost fifty years whole districts were levelled to make place for new construction. Leopold II began his career as a builder by constructing a bedroom fountain and ended it with a triumphal arch. Despite his building frenzy, it would not be right to compare him to that other mad royal builder, King Louis of Bavaria, whose fairy-tale castles and country residences seem like romantic opera settings. King Louis indulged himself, but King Leopold was concerned about the beautification of his country. Brussels owes most of its grandeur to the king. Without him, it would have remained a provincial backwater.

Anyway, Leopold wasn't quite as mad as his father thought he was. As a young man, he proved surprisingly well informed about the intricacies of Belgian politics and frequently spoke on the subject in the Senate. He wanted to transform Brussels and turn it into a prestigious metropolis, whatever the cost. Why did he want to do this? His desire to metamorphose the city dated from his early youth. In his childhood Brussels was a dull town. His mother, Queen Louise-Marie, a French princess, would often complain about the dullness of Brussels. She thought Brussels was narrow-minded, small and lifeless and felt that a town like that was not suitable for someone

of her elevated rank. In a sense she was right. Brussels did not have imposing boulevards or large castles. By French standards Place Royale and Place des Martyrs were modest little squares. In addition, there was hardly any society life. The Saxe-Coburg dynasty ruled over a tiny country singularly lacking in grandeur, which the Queen found deplorable. It must have been the subject of many heated discussions at the royal dinner-table, which probably helped the young prince Leopold decide that he would have to do something about it eventually.

Consequently, he had many monumental buildings constructed throughout the country and a large number of parks and tree-lined avenues laid out. Only now, towards the end of the 20th century, are we beginning to learn again that a great deal of ugliness can be effectively concealed by using screens of trees. Leopold opened up medieval Brussels by building wide avenues and new suburbs. Brussels became the true heart of the young kingdom. In order to suppress the anti-Belgian sentiments that lingered for a long time both in Flanders and Wallonia, the streets and squares of the capital were filled with memorials. Sculptors and bronze-moulders were set to work and created many surprisingly beautiful monuments.

Leopold dressed Brussels in a coat of greenery – he surrounded the city centre with a multitude of parks. He also enlarged the palace grounds at Laeken and had wide avenues laid out. By putting pressure on the local authorities, he indirectly contributed to the extension of Avenue Louise, the building of the Palais de Justice, the laying out of Parc du Cinquantenaire and the expropriation of Mont des Arts. But not everything he did had a salutary effect on Brussels. His treatment of the old working-class districts in the inner city was rather cavalier and he met with

strong opposition from burgomaster Charles Buls, Brussels' most famous conservationist.

The King was a shrewd businessman. When from 1896 onwards the trade in ivory and rubber from the Congo, which as a Crown Dominion came under his personal control, began to yield considerable profits and money began to pour in, the King grew immensely rich and was able to realise his boyhood dreams without the interference of others. But he did not commit himself openly and often worked through intermediaries whenever it seemed appropriate. This he did, for instance, in order to have the triumphal arch in Parc du Cinquantenaire built – which the king meant as a present for his seventy-fifth birthday. The country did not have enough money to pay for the arch, so the king paid for it out of his own funds, giving money to sponsors who in turn donated the arch to the country...The arch has little artistic value, being rather pompous and old-fashioned, even for the time when it was built, at the beginning of this century. The king was also behind the laying-out of Avenue de Tervuren, Avenue du Parc Royale, Avenue de Meysse, and Boulevard du Souverain. In addition he had two palaces built, one in Parc de Warande and another in Laeken, both rivalling the splendour of Buckingham Palace. Alphonse Balat, his favourite architect, was given free rein. Horta said of Balat that he was 'the most classicist of all classicist architects'. Quite so, for Balat detested new ideas and looked to the past for inspiration. Both the king and his architect were partial to eighteenth-century French Classicism. Consequently, the architect designed huge stairwells and ballrooms with towering pillars and soaring walls. His works are a delight to see, but perhaps a trifle too solid and too overbearing. Balat's masterpiece are the huge greenhouses in the Laeken palace grounds, commissioned by King Leopold, who was a keen gardener. The greenhouses were built in the 1870s and 1880s. Their many cupolas make them look somewhat like a Byzantine cathedral. They were quite avant-garde at the time when they were built because of their exotic shape and glass-and-iron construction. They are among the oldest and most beautiful greenhouses of Europe. Once a year they are open to visitors, a delight for flower lovers and architecture fans. Leopold II loved these buildings so much that he had a small house built next to it. He insisted on every night checking the temperature in the greenhouses himself. He finally died in his beloved garden. Behind the Laeken palace are the two quaintest buildings in Brussels – the Japanese Tower and the Chinese Pavilion. The king had them built early this century. The tower was, in fact, shipped partly from Yokohama, and the furniture of the Chinese Pavilion, originally a restaurant, came from Shanghai.

King Leopold II was a despot with a vision. He realised, long before others did, that Brussels was far too small. At the beginning of his reign the city was confined to tight medieval bounds. The king created new monumental edifices on the edge of the city, necessitating a ring road from which grand boulevards branched off. His finest creation, partly paid for by his own money, is Avenue de Tervuren. Near Parc de Woluwe this magnificent avenue merges with the natural landscape to re-emerge again near the Central Africa Museum. The king managed to combine the ingenuity of baron Haussmann, the architect of Paris, with the romanticism of English landscaped gardens.

These grand avenues and parks are his greatest inheritance. In the early part of this century a new city developed around them. Along the south-eastern edge from Uccle to Schaerbeek young architects

created a new, contemporary architecture. Using small idyllic parks as their points of reference, they built beautiful houses for the rich in exuberant designs, based on a mixture of neo-styles, Art Nouveau and early Modernism. These miscellaneous creations are an open-air museum of early twentieth-century architecture. Recognition of their achievement has been slow, but it seems likely that in the near future more and more tourists will visit these suburbs, rather than the damaged heart of the old city.

City plans show that these districts are centred on green spots, small parks like oases of peace and beauty, which have their roots in a distant past forgotten by everyone. Formerly a small brook, called the Maalbeek, ran through this part of Brussels. From its source in the Foret de Soignes it passed through Ixelles, Etterbeek, Saint-Josse-ten-Noode and Schaerbeek. The brook got its name from the many water mills along its banks. Its waters supplied fifty fishponds, lined with leather manufactories, country homes and inns, where the bourgeoisie would go on Sundays to enjoy a glass of Belgian beer. Virtually nothing remains of this pastoral scenery, except the small parks. The oldest is in Quartier Leopold, just off Parc de Bruxelles. This is where the first suburb was built last century, after the city walls had been pulled down. The moneyed classes, landowners and industrialists, like John Cockerill, had imposing mansions built here. Few of them are left, and most have been replaced by office blocks, a transformation that has turned Quartier Leopold, right around he corner from the EU's headquarters, into one of the least interesting parts of Brussels.

Parc Leopold was originally a zoo, designed by Alphonse Balat. In 1853 Balat built a huge glass greenhouse for a giant lily, just two years after the first World Fair in Crystal Palace, when this type of archi-

tecture was first used for large structures. The zoo was a failure and it was closed in 1876. Balat's ingenious metal work of art was then moved to the botanical gardens of Meysse, where it still is. At the turn of the century Parc Leopold became a scientific centre. Various university departments moved here, including those of sociology, health care and anatomy. They were housed in beautiful buildings with an industrial design marked by the use of cast iron. The Science Museum, where dinosaurs are on show among painted pillars, has an especially opulent setting.

Long before the dinos arrived, an artist lived in this neighbourhood whose pictures were of prehistoric size. They were so large that most people find them rather too much of a good thing. They are not exactly masterpieces either. But Antoine Wiertz (1806-1865), as the artist was called, never for one moment doubted his own genius. His studio in a dark corner of Parc Leopold is now threatened by the EU's headquarters. Ironically, it was built with government money. Heaven knows how Wiertz managed to wheedle the money for his studio out of the state. The studio is very large, as it had to be in order to provide room for his huge paintings. His masterpiece, picturing the Greeks and Trojans fighting over the body of Patrocles, measures no less than sixteen by thirteen feet. And it is not even his largest work. Wiertz considered himself to be at least the equal of Rubens. Most people disagreed. He met with a fair amount of success in Italy, but Paris turned him down. He then naïvely planned to turn Brussels into the capital of Europe and reduce Paris to an insignificant provincial town. Hardly could he have foreseen that one day the heart of the European Community would beat in his rear garden.

It was in Schaerbeek that the Maalbeek must have presented its most beautiful aspect, for the

The cemeteries of Brussels are, as it were, open-air museums. A fine example is Laeken cemetery, which is the Belgian equivalent of Père Lachaise. This is the last resting place of the Belgian monarchs, along with many artists and politicians. The gravestones in fact reflect the architecture of the city, and a number of renowned architects, including Horta, designed tombstones. As a result, the

short stretch of it that survived used to be compared to the Josaphat Valley in the Holy Land. The resemblance was first noticed four hundred years ago by a pilgrim returning from Palestine. This explains the name of Parc Josaphat, situated in a fairly low-lying valley and cut off from the world by roads and skyscrapers. Schaerbeek's reputation has suffered because of the several unsafe neighbourhoods in the

district. This is regrettable, for much of its Belle Epoque architecture has been excellently preserved. Parc Josaphat is lined by many imposing houses. The new suburbs were built in a very short time, for even a century ago both Schaerbeek and Saint-Josse-ten-Noode were mere rural villages. They were part of an area that functioned as the market garden of Brussels, producing both vegetables and fruit. In a few

short years all the fruit growers, market gardeners and wine-farmers had gone. The new suburbs were completed in 1895. The old villages had been razed, even the village church and the layout of the streets had gone. They were replaced by a new main street, Avenue Louis Bertrand, where tall townhouses were built. Architects were invited to submit designs, and this led to fierce competition between traditional and modern architects, including such famous practitioners as Gustave Strauwen and Henri Jacobs, who flirted with the whiplash style, and Louis de la Censerie, who favoured pompous Neo-Renaissance designs.

Leopold II became involved as well, although he contributed greenery rather than stone. At the time Parc Josaphat was still private property, and the lady

entire range of architectural styles can be seen in evidence in these cemeteries, from neo-Gothic to Egyptomania. Certain styles betoken the philosophical persuasion of the deceased. As well as Laeken, the cemeteries of Evere, Saint Giles and Uccle-Dieweg are well worth a visit.

Sand for the Rich

You will need to be patient if you want to really discover Brussels as the picturesque spots are not within easy reach. This panoramic view from the town hall of Saint Giles shows a view of the variegated cityscape as far as the eye can see. There is certainly a lot to admire, but you cannot stay just near Grand'Place. Not far from there, for example, you will discover Sablon, one of the best-preserved districts of the city with many restaurants and antique dealers. Beyond the inner Brussels ring-road, you will find a suburb which around the turn of the century was teeming with fine houses built in eclectic styles.

THE HILTON building on Boulevard de Waterloo hides a secret. Few people know that behind this concrete colossus there is a charming little park, whose intimate character just seems to call out for a leisurely stroll. But the place is empty – no-one goes here except cats, chasing birds. Anyone wanting to get away from the bustle of Boulevard de Waterloo should keep an eye out for the gate leading to Egmont Palace. It is easy to overlook, as is only proper. Otherwise the narrow passageway it opens onto would cease to be a real discovery. At the end of the passageway is an old-fashioned park, laid out along the former medieval fortifications, traces of which can still be seen in the slightly differing soil levels. To the right is Egmont Palace, which was meant as a summer residence and really shouldn't have been in the city at all. It has a run-down orangery, where for the past fifty years not a single orange has been grown. Old prints show that many centuries ago there used to be a kind of French garden with low hedges here, at the time when Brussels was the capital of the Low Countries. The park gives an indication of the large size of the private gardens of the aristocracy that used to be common in this part of the city.

The park is our point of departure for a tour of Sablon, the most charming part of Brussels. The very name has a magic sound. It refers to the white sands of the hill on which the upper town was built and where the aristocracy used to live, near the ducal palace. Last century, when the lower town was completely restyled, the remaining aristocrats moved to modern houses on Boulevard Maurice Lemonnier and Boulevard Anspach. Within a few decades Sablon was transformed. All the craftsmen and merchants moved away to be replaced by antique and art dealers. Delicatessens and fashion shops were other newcomers.

Sablon is a good area for a stroll, for it is one of the few Brussels districts that have been saved from the wholesale demolition of the 'sixties. Even so, in Rue des Laines we find waste lots among eighteenth-century buildings. It is a sad sight, for this street is among the most beautiful of Brussels. I believe that the De Mérode mansion is the oldest house in Rue des Laines. In the eighteenth century it was home to the count of Bournonville. When the ministers of Empress Maria Theresia came to Brussels they would stay here. Its Renaissance red-brick and white-chalk façade shows that the origin of the house goes back to a far earlier time.

Before the bombardment of 1695 Flemish Renaissance was the predominant style of building in the city. Afterwards, the bourgeoisie living near Sablon had their houses rebuilt according to modern fashions. The colourful façades were covered by plaster and the saddle roofs replaced by Mansard roofs. It is likely that far more old masonry has been preserved than can be seen with the naked eye from the street. Whenever houses are pulled down, bright red brick walls re-emerge.

Further along Rue des Laines we come across Egmont Palace with its charming front. After the death of count Lamoraal Egmont, who together with count Hoorn was beheaded on Grand'Place in 1568, by order of King Philip II, his palace became the property of the Arenberg family. In 1753 they had a beautiful wing added in Classicist style, designed by the architect Servandoni. Further additions in the same style followed, creating an imposing ensemble that is strikingly different from the prevailing architecture in this neighbourhood.

In Parc du Petit Sablon counts Egmont and Hoorn can be met in person. They stand in the middle of a pond, amidst a lot of greenery and flanked by

Petit Sablon (previous page) is a cosy spot bedecked with greenery and graced with elegant statues and stately buildings. Of course, it is just beside the Egmont Palace, whose façade, designed by Servandoni, can be seen from the park. The public garden is the creation of the architect Hendrik Beyaert and his pupil Paul Hankar and dates from the end of the last century. To complete his design, the architect certainly did his homework, consulting old documents, engravings and paintings to give the park its ancient feel. However, it is a purely romantic creation. In the middle of the park stand the sculptures of Counts Egmont and Hoorn, who were executed in 1568 on Grand'Place by order of Philip II. The two counts are surrounded by famous scientists, among then Ortelius, Mercator and Dodoens. But the most striking feature of the park is the trellis work on which there are 48 sculptures representing artisans. These additional decorative features were in fact made by no fewer than twenty-two sculptors.

statues of famous contemporaries such as Marnix van Sint-Aldegonde, Abraham Ortelius, Gerard Mercator, Rembert Dodoens and William the Silent. It seems highly doubtful that these dignitaries would have been willing to strike such a brotherly pose during their lifetime. This romantic park was designed by Hendrik Beyaert and Paul Hankar, who was reponsible for the wrought-iron ornaments. It is an early example of the Art Nouveau designs of Brussels. The park is screened off by trellis work, crowned by statues representing forty-eight different crafts. The designs are by the painter Xavier Mellery, but the exquisitely crafted sculptures are the work of the best contemporary Belgian artists. They included De Vigne, Dillens, Lambeaux and Van der Stappen. The peaceful atmosphere in this park is not just caused by all the greenery. Whenever traffic noise ceases a prelude by Liszt or a polonaise by Chopin can be heard in the distance. Music prevails here, for adjacent to the park are a conservatoire and a richly-endowed Museum of Musical Instruments.

Both the park and the Sablon church are part of a major urban plan that was completed by the end of last century. In order to create an elegant link with the Palais de Justice Rue de la Régence was built across the Sablon district. This street runs like a straight line through the medieval area. In order to build this new street Rue Montagne de la Cour had to be pulled down. The Museé des Beaux-Arts has replaced several picturesque lanes that used to link the lower and the upper town. The only remainder of this earlier period is Rue de Ruysbroeck, in a valley behind Place du Grand Sablon. This obscure street with its fine houses is like a breath of fresh air.

The large-scale demolitions created Mont des Arts, which used to be far more charming than it is now. Its Third Reich architecture, in the words of the writer Geert van Istendael, has made this the most desolate part of the city. The large townhouses near the Sablon church were all pulled down, including that of the Thurn and Taxis family. This aristocratic family controlled the postal services of the Hapsburg empire, a monopoly which made them very rich. Their sumptuous tomb is in the Sablon church.

At the turn of the century the church itself was redesigned. Old pictures show how picturesque it used to be. It had never been completely finished, and its restoration was carried out with such zeal that virtually the entire exterior was restyled. Romantic as it may be, the Sablon church can thus hardly be called an authentic medieval building.

Place du Grand Sablon on the slope of the hill creates a special visual effect – it is like a stairway leading to the church. Saturday mornings are the most pleasant time of the week to enjoy the relaxed atmosphere here. On that day the antique dealers and restaurants prepare to welcome their many visitors. From early in the morning sturdy men carry antiques to the stalls around the church, where an interesting open-air antiques market is held every week. Don't expect to find any precious antiques here, the objects on sale are mainly a better class of second-hand goods. People looking for the real thing are well-advised to wander around the square, where antique dealers are plentiful. It is amazing that so many of them can be found in a small metropolis like Brussels. They offer a large variety of wares. Nowadays many of them specialise in decorative objects. Some dealers concentrate on old Flemish art. Many others sell mainly African art, a reminder of the Belgian presence in Congo. Even in the pre-war years ethnic art was available here. It is not surprising that Brussels is the international centre of the trade in African art.

The antique trade of Sablon branches out to the city centre. By way of Rue Lebeau you descend to Grand'Place. Antique shops are plentiful in this area. Going west, in the direction of the imposing Palais de Justice, we arrive at Place du Jeu de Balle in the Marolles, the most famous working-class area of Brussels. This square is the scene of a daily flea-market. Even traders come here, looking for bargains. They will arrive early in the morning, round about six thirty, on weekdays, for during weekends all prices are doubled for the 'benefit' of people from out of town. People go to Place du Jeu de Balle for finds and for its atmosphere. The large crowds and the quantities of cheap trinkets create the illusion of

Sablon is of course the favourite haunt of those who like to browse among antiques, especially during the weekend when an interesting antiques market takes place around the church. Antiques are sold just about everywhere in the district. A little further on, towards the Marolles, you can visit Place du Jeu de Balle, where a flea-market is held every day.

an Arab bazaar. Lining the square are many shops selling second-hand goods. This used to be an area of craftshops. Only a very few are left. In Rue des Tanneurs we still find De Fluiter, who specialise in old copperware, and in Rue des Capucines there is De Backer weaver's shop, famous throughout the world for its lace and braid.

Sablon, then, marks the boundary between the upper and lower town, beteen rich and poor. East of Sablon we get to the royal district, dominated by the magnificent Place Royale. This was once the site of Coudenberg palace, one of Europe's most beautiful fortresses. First it was the residence of the dukes of Brabant, then of the dukes of Burgundy, then of Philip the Good, and finally of the Emperor Charles and Albert and Isabella. It was the political heart of the Southern Netherlands. But the castle was destroyed by fire in 1731. Its remains were pulled down and the hill on which it stood was levelled. Consequently, the soil still contains a lot of interesting things. Archeologists are now digging up the *aula magna*, the main assembly hall of the palace, whose remains are largely covered by the cobbles of Place Royale.

From the castle people must have had a breathtaking view of the lower town. They would have been able to see elegant façades, many church towers, the slim City Hall spire and quite a lot of greenery. Albrecht Dürer once admired and described this view. Place Royale now looks totally different from what it looked in the past. Hardly anything from the past has remained, except for a small part of Hôtel Ravenstein in Rue Ravenstein and the Nassau chapel of 1520, now imprisoned in the concrete abomination that is the National Library.

When in the 1760s the Austrian Netherlands were booming, the governor, Charles of Lorraine,

wanted to enhance the allure of his residential city. He had a small palace built behind the Nassau chapel and asked a French architect to design a grand square on the empty site of the former castle. Bernabé Guimard, the architect, started work in 1769. He used the Place Royale in Reims, which is very similar, as his model. The new square was dressed in a Classicist costume, with very formal, monumental façades, many pillars and overbearing cornices. Three decades after the first excavations at Pompey, this had become the fashionable style of building. It was a stark contrast with the opulent Baroque ornamentation of Grand'Place.

Round about the same time a similar project was carried out in the inner city, where Place des Martyrs was being built. Its architect, Claude Fisco, was a descendant of the Genoese Fiesque family, and modelled his design on Greek architecture. But he was less inclined to monumentalism than Guimard and the houses he built were meant for private residence. His archtectural style makes clear that Fisco was a genuine Brabander. In all its military simplicity Place des Martyrs reminds us of the intimate character of old Baroque Brussels.

Charles of Lorraine obviously preferred to stay aloof from the city. From Place Royale and the adjacent park the medieval city centre could hardly be seen at all. Nowadays the view has changed, because many buildings have been pulled down, but originally the square was an isolated little island, as befitted the segregated society of olden times. In fact, Charles' layouts were as futuristic as the Paris district of La Défense is in our days. He had the Austrian landscape designer Joachim Zinner draw straight streets, lined by towering buildings. His design was not just futuristic but also determined the future appearance of the town, little though Charles or Zinner may have

In the middle of the last century, the south of the city was undergoing major construction work. The architect Joseph Poelaert added what was in fact the jewel in the crown, the colossal Palais de Justice, which was erected between 1866 and 1883. This enormous monument highlighted the contrast between rich and poor because it in fact overlooks the Marolles, which was once one of the poorest districts in Brussels. Moreover, at the time, the construction was not admired by everyone. On 15 October 1883, the inauguration ceremony was seriously disrupted by poor people who set about damaging the furniture. Furthermore, many dignitaries believed this project was a complete waste of money. It was one of the most imposing buildings in Europe, and was even slightly larger than St. Peter's Basilica in Rome. In terms of proportion and style, the Palais de Justice is a far cry from the avant-garde architecture that was to come into vogue just after its construction. Over a hundred years later, the building is much more beautiful than ever, and with its fine patina the entrance hall is truly reminiscent of a Roman monument.

45

realised it. A few decades later the new streets became the framework for a further extension of the town. Arterial roads were built across Brussels, running from the Palais de Justice to Schaerbeek and from the Parliament to beyond Parc du Cinquantenaire.

But to return to Parc de Bruxelles, once the site of tournaments organised by the local dukes. Zinner redesigned the old ducal garden which dated from 1773, by using a modern, French concept. His intention was to create a promenade for the upper ten. The groundplan he drew was shaped like a pair of compasses, a Masonic symbol. This was no surprise, as the Governor was a Free Mason himself. The Warande, as the park is sometimes referred to, was to rival the Champs Elysées in Paris and Hyde Park in London.

Zinner's creation seems very modern. The straight avenues are purely French in design. This was quite usual at the time, but in between them are undulating little landscapes, designed according to the latest English fashions. The most interesting thing about this slightly derelict park are its many statues. Among them are eighteenth-century treasures from the ducal garden. The most exciting and mysterious part of the park, in the north, contains several old buildings, including the ancient Théâtre du Parc, behind which can be seen the remains of the former Café Velloni, where aristocratic ladies would go to enjoy a cup of coffee. And to listen to music, for early this century a music theatre, the Waux Hall, was built here for that purpose. This charming *bonbonnière* was fully restored by Baron Eric d'Huart. We shall return to it later for a better look.

Behind Doors and Windows

Behind the façades of Brussels we discover a convivial and surprising city. Sometimes it seems as if Brussels has a stronger appeal to foreigners than to the inhabitants themselves. They admire the extraordinary houses and enjoy the surrealistic atmosphere – this is where people like Brueghel, Magritte, Horta and Van de Velde lived under a single roof.

One
with the City

I T IS HARD TO IMAGINE THAT FIVE HUNDRED years ago Brussels was a large city. Some landmarks, like the town hall and the cathedral, do betray a certain grandeur, but several other smaller towns can boast of huge churches and massive fortifications. The thing about Brussels is that the town lacks medieval houses. And yet, there must have been many houses built during the Middle Ages. By 1480 Brussels had a population of more than 45,000. At that time, the town centre must have been at least as busy as Grand'Place is now in summertime. Not only did Brussels undergo many transformations, its population changed as well. Sometimes with regrettable results, for the inner city is now thinly populated. This may be difficult to understand, for quite a large number of beautiful historical houses have been left empty. Shopping centres and office blocks have driven out the merchants and the small workshops. The few remaining residential houses have fallen into disrepair. Even so, an increasing number of people are now beginning to move back to the inner city. On our trip through Brussels we shall encounter many exciting houses, whose fascination derives from their beauty and location.

For instance, in Parc de Bruxelles, between the Royal Palace and Parliament, we discover an open-air theatre, the Waux Hall. Baron Eric d'Huart is patiently and skilfully restoring it from its former ruinous state. Full restoration will take many years, but he has already moved in and feels very happy in his new home, which is hidden among the greenery behind the Théâtre du Parc. The first Waux Hall was built on this spot in 1780. This type of park building originated in England, where in the seventeenth century Earl Breauté, nicknamed 'Faulk', used to organise entertainments in his gardens, known as the Vaux Hall Gardens. They served as the model for other

The secret of Parc de Bruxelles is hidden behind the Théâtre du Parc, where baron Eric d'Huart has found a haven in the old Waux Hall. He has transformed what used to be a ruin into a splendid home.

Waux Halls – as they came to be known – that were built two centuries ago in Brussels, Spa and Paris. The Brussels Waux Halls consisted of a theatre, a coffeehouse and a ballroom. Books, jewelry, perfumes and prints were on sale as well. The buildings were repeatedly renovated. Baron d'Huart's Waux Hall was built in 1913 and was the most recent addition to the original complex. It was just a small open-air theatre with a large stage and backstage and dressing-rooms for the actors. Because of the outbreak of World War I in 1914 it was never actually used. Gradually it fell into disrepair. 'I was the fairy-tale baron who came to kiss the sleeping beauty awake after 70 years,' says Eric d'Huart with a smile. 'But actually it required more than just a kiss, for we had to turn a building that was never meant for private residence into a home. The interior was not allowed to be too theatrical. A theatrical setting is fun, but it is not suitable for daily use.'

The building was turned into a spacious home with enough room to live and work. As a restorer of art objects, Eric d'Huart needs a lot of space. Downstairs we encounter a 'clinic for old chandeliers', filled with various parts of chandeliers. The next room is a plaster workshop where decorative ornaments are moulded. And there is a cellar to stock candles, for d'Huart uses no fewer than four thousand candles every three months! The house is full of chandeliers. The most beautiful specimens are in a small sitting-room. They are precious girandoles mounted with rock-crystal pearls, made for Coco Chanel by a Spanish designer. Once they lighted her apartment in Rue Faubourg Saint-Honoré in Paris. This mysterious room also contains several old-fashioned Turkish sofas, which are charming rather than beautiful. 'They are really examples of old-fashioned kitsch,' says Eric d'Huart. They help to offset the

53

Making this former open-air theatre into a house was no mean task. After all, no one had ever lived in the building before. In addition, the decor had to be simple and unadorned. In the words of the baron, theatre decor is all right for a one-off event, but not to live in every day. The architecture is indeed very simple, but the adornments are truly opulent. However, by no means everything in this house is quite so costly, but with a dark palette of colours, subdued lighting and touches of gold, the master of the house has created something of a mysterious hermitage.

atmosphere of distinction in the room. The main room radiates a festive mood because of its several Venetian chandeliers. They are new, but were modelled on old ones hanging in the Ca'Rezzonico in Venice, a palace the baron has fallen in love with. On the walls are decorative paintings, from a mansion in Namur. They display strawberries, a fruit that has brought many riches to the region. The baron literally saved these charming trinkets when they were on the point of being put out with the trash.

The main reason why Baron d'Huart has chosen to live here is the location of Waux Hall. 'I have a 24-acre garden, at times all to myself,' he says. Besides, the Parc de Bruxelles is a tribute to the age of Mozart, the age of the Enlightenment, an era highly appreciated by the baron.

Waux Hall is being restored step-by-step. At the moment the final touches are put to the trellises that used to cover the entire building. They are a typical French decoration, which used to be very popular for gazebos. Whenever he can, baron d'Huart uses craftsmen with traditional skills. It is a fascinating idea that on the eve of the new millennium it is still possible to find – albeit with some effort – many craftsmen whose skills are just the same as those of their predecessors who worked many centuries ago. In that sense Baron d'Huart's home is also a tribute to the skills of the past.

Between the Royal Palace and the Parliament, in an inconspicuous corner of the Warande Park, you may come across this splendid bonbonnière. This monument is in fact known to very few people as it is hidden from the street by a screen of time-honoured trees. Baron d'Huart has the park to himself in the evening. This is a splendid veranda that goes back to the days of Mozart. It was built during the Austrian period, that is the late eighteenth century. Five pathways with a triangular motif traverse the groundplan, and some see in this the representation of a pair of compasses, which is a Masonic symbol.

Architects: VDVH & ASSOC,
Johan Van Dessel in cooperation with
Jose Van Hee. Date: 1986/1990.

Here we get a peek at Philip L'Evêque's pied-à-terre while he sits quietly reading. In Brussels' heyday in the second half of the last century, when it was the capital of a rich industrial hinterland, large mansions were built along splendid avenues. The finest decorators were commissioned to embellish these fine houses. This was one such mansion, the winter residence of a noble family from Ghent. A few picturesque traces remain of the sumptuous decor.

JUST OVER 130 YEARS AGO BURGOMASTER Anspach of Brussels realised his life's work, the construction of a new residential district on top of the River Senne, in between the Bourse and Gare du Midi. In this way the rich took over a large part of the medieval slums of Brussels. The picturesque streets and narrow lanes were destroyed and replaced by straight avneues lined by tall houses. Nowadays all this showiness has fallen into ruin. In this run-down environment we come across an artistic home. Behind a peeling façade in Rue du Midi we encounter the rough-and-ready interior where Claude Terryn and Philippe L'Evêque live.

'Rather than carry out an exact restoration, we decided to create an interior with an atmosphere of decay,' says Philippe. They removed the wallpaper so that the original decorations re-emerged, which even in their damaged state are strikingly sophisticated. Formerly the walls were covered with frames of precious woven cloth. There used to be charming supraportas over the doors. The only parts of the furnishings that were well-preserved are the mantelpieces. They were exceptionally well finished in types of marble that are no longer available. This huge house was built around 1867 for a noble family from Ghent, who would stay here in winter to enjoy the many entertainments offered by the capital. They lived a stone's throw away from the financial and cultural heart of Brussels, for the Théâtre de la Monnaie is very near. It was a time when Belgium was flourishing, with a booming industry in both Wallonia and Flanders. While the workers toiled the wealthy bourgeoisie would lean back in an easy chair or a voltaire to enjoy a fragrant cigar.

When Claude and Philippe moved in most of the beauty of the house had gone. It was in a very sorry state. They opted for an adventurous refurbishing in

line with their life style. They redecorated their apartment with an eye to the fashions popular in the 1870s, when neo-styles were much sought after and designers were very keen on a mixture of styles. The interior now displays a modern translation of this approach. At first stylistic confusion seems to reign. A modern table, designed by Pascal Bauwens, is the showpiece of the living room. There are also pre-war lamps designed by Jean Prouvé and a genuine Le Corbusier chaise-longue. A Biedermeier landscape is the centrepiece of Claude's office. He achieved a rather surrealistic effect by putting the large painting on top of the mantelpiece. His favourite work of art, a pen-and-ink drawing by Philippe Jullian, is concealed behind the door. This is an object of considerable interest to connoisseurs. An essay-writer who published many articles about interior design, Jullian was a frequent contributor to *Connaissance des Arts*. His drawings are very rare and much in demand. Claude found this treasure at a neighbour's! The house contains yet other striking works of art, such as an original plaster study by Jean-Baptiste Carpeaux, one of the leading figures of French Romanticism. But Claude also likes curios. He has a modest collection of serving-trays from famous hotels and resturants, including the Metropole in Brussels and the Moulin Rouge in Paris. It is truly a home full of contrasts.

These contrasts are even manifested in the architecture itself, for the open groundplan with a series of interlinking rooms creates the illusion of a country home, even though the house is set in the heart of the city. When all the doors are open the apartment turns into a large festive hall, where people can forget about the chaos outside.

In the year of our Lord 1867, when this property was built, Napoleon III was wielding absolute power in France, and many French intellectuals and artists found themselves in Brussels as exiles. While the city became richer and richer, poverty was still in evidence in the back streets. However, here in this miniature palace, there is no trace of any poverty. What we see instead is a distinguished decor without a hint of modernism. It should not be forgotten that at the time William Morris was

exploring quite new avenues. This cocoon is actually a thinly-disguised ode to the Ancien Régime. The decoration now to be found there is contemporary, debonair and full of humour and refreshing contrasts. We also find an old Corbusier armchair and a pen-and-ink drawing by Jullian on the wall. This nonchalance is something we can enjoy, but it should not be thought that everything has been left to chance. Indeed, every object is the fruit of painstaking research.

The stately Galeries St Hubert are not only among the most pleasant haunts in the city where the beau monde can stroll at their leisure. People actually live above these olde-worlde shops and cafes. In fact, the flats in the arcade are very well protected from the elements by the glass roof. Furthermore, the distinction between interior and exterior is rather blurred. The monumental decor, the fine shops and the cosy coffee houses – along with the presence of the inhabitants – make this microcosm a real village within the city. It is no wonder that a hundred years ago this arcade, during the winter time, was the favourite meeting-place of the French exiles who had come to Belgium to escape the clutches of Napoleon III.

IN THE GALERIES ST HUBERT one is hardly aware of the seasons, because it always seems like summer here, thanks to the glass roof that lets through even the tiniest ray of sunlight. There is always a pervasive quiet in this magnificent arcade because traffic noise is shut out and the only thing that can be heard are people's footsteps – and occasionally the tunes of street musicians. Nowadays violin players from Eastern Europe are often making music on the corner of Rue des Bouchers. Their melancholy tunes enhance the atmosphere even further. As if such enhancement were needed in this architectural paradise. In order to be able to relish the atmosphere Danny Beun, a window display designer, usually leaves his own windows open. His second-floor apartment is just below the glass ceiling. Most people don't know there are so many private residences in Galeries St Hubert. In fact, there are seventy apartments over the shops. Spacious flats take up the first floor, servants's quarters the second.

The arcade always reminds Danny Beun of a village, for most of the residents know each other. They form rather a special community, because many of them are architects, designers, photographers or artists. The basements below the arcade contain the oldest power station in the country. The arcade was the first building to replace gas by electricity – showing the care that goes into the maintenance of the building. The arcade management in fact employs a number of people to take care of the upkeep of the buildings. Sadly, the rest of the district is rather derelict, as exemplified by a series of beautiful but run-down townhouses stretching from the arcade to the Théâtre de la Monnaie.

Danny Beun has helped to preserve the arcade by carrying out a first-class refurbishing of his own apartment. He has aimed for authenticity. Even the

old glass in the windows was preserved. Each room has been given a different colour scheme. The passage and the dining room – in use as a living room – seem rather austere, because of the very light colouring of the walls and the scarcity of furniture. The most remarkable and intimate room is the small sitting room with its deliberately old-fashioned atmosphere, which allows Beun to forget about daily routines. The centrepiece of the room is a large mahogany sofa made from an old bed. The decorative volutes of the sofa are mirrored in the murals. In the Brussels fleamarket Beun found a suitable chandelier and a sconce. Together with the folded drapes they evoke the past, when Galeries St Hubert were still the favourite meeting-place of Victor Hugo, Charles Baudelaire and Alexandre Dumas.

61

THIS HOUSE IS LIKE AN OLD SHIP WHICH, somewhat weather-beaten after many voyages around the world, has finally found a mooring-place in the old harbour. It has dropped anchor behind Rue de la Cigogne, near old Rue de Flandre, the former trade route from Bruges and Cologne, where for many centuries goods were hauled from and into the city. A bit further along you can walk across the filled-in docks next to Eglise Sainte Catherine. This entire neighbourhood was shaped by water, ships, horses and carts. Now, behind Rue Dansaert, the area is rather desolate. Recently, artists and fashion designers have found places to live in this neighbourhood, which is now seeing a return to its old conviviality.

The resemblance to a ship is striking, for when the door opens and scarce light shines in the hallway you seem to find yourself between two decks. A narrow stairway leads to the upper deck. Upstairs you get to the hull, or at least that is what the roof-beams make you think of. The entire house has become lopsided, rather like the interiors painted by Vincent Van Gogh, where all the lines clash with reality. The wooden floor slants, creating a distorted perspective. Some of the floorboards have come loose, so that the ark of antique dealer Daniël Schaffeneers seems to float on water. All this creates a peaceful atmosphere, quite a blessing in the heart of Brussels.

Schaffeneers likes houses that show signs of wear and tear. He feels attracted by imperfections. In addition, this house has an eventful history, as the curved beams testify. It must have been built shortly after the French bombardment of 1695, when the greater part of Brussels was destroyed. The house was rebuilt with materials taken from destroyed houses. This is obvious from the – somewhat over-heavy – beams in the reception room. Nothing was wasted in those days. The craftsmen were keen to make a profit. Such recycling helped to create an artless picturesqueness. Many expensive materials were thus transferred from the rich to the poor, for instance the eighteenth-century floor in the hallway, which was taken from a far richer townhouse.

Daniël Schaffeneers carefully restored his house. First he removed everything superfluous, such as wallpaper and plaster. Then he created a large living room and a terrace. The walls were given an old patina and the beams were distempered with Spanish white, an ordinary, old-fashioned whitening that can easily be washed off. Surprisingly few modern amenities were installed during refurbishment. The bath and the washing basin are from a London house and the kitchen closet is from a farmhouse near Namur. It is only to be expected that an antique dealer will re-use antiques. It is perhaps less to be expected that this will create a harmonious ensemble. But everything matches, despite the mixture of styles. Schaffeneers is a past-master at this sort of thing. With Jean-Claude Jacquemart he runs *Atmosphère*, a superb antique shop on Sablon. Their business often takes them on trips around the world, which explains Daniël's fascination with British colonial style. At least once a year he visits India. By using local transport he gets to even the smallest villages where many beautiful objects can still be found.

The showpiece in the living room is from Boston. It is a tall mahogany cupboard that originally belonged to a haberdashers. Around this piece of furniture Schaffeneers created a colonial decor by using an old-fashioned Napoleon III couch and by covering the walls with Chinese calligraphy. He likes painting, though his preference is for exotic rather than traditional western painting. Also on the wall is a Chinese glass painting, bought in Malaysia.

In a corner of his reception room is an antique iron bed, also bought in Malaysia. This may not seem the most logical place for such a piece of furniture, but it is well-chosen. This is his guestroom. The house is to small to have a spare bedroom, so the bed was put here.

The kitchen and dining room are at the rear of the house and seem distinctly rural. There are wicker baskets, rural furniture and earthenware. Simple designs and cheerful colours abound. Originally, Schaffeneers meant to furnish the entire house in this style, but he never got round to doing so. 'When I moved in,' he says, 'I realised I had many amusing possessions I could not bear to leave behind.' As he was unable to decide in favour of one particular interior, he created two totally different interiors. 'You can't just throw all of your stuff away', he says. 'Antique dealers are stuck with a particular heritage.' Not that he minds, for he loves the objects he has surrounded himself with and does not want to sell them.

Antique dealer Daniel Schaffeneers has lovingly restored his house and filled it with souvenirs from many far-flung places. The antique bed and the Chinese glass paintings are trouvailles from Malaysia. Around the bed, he has made a tiny guests' room in the middle of the living room. At the top of the house, under the roof trusses, we find the bathroom. The kitchen – with a dining area – is tucked away at the back of the house. Using an old door and a fragment of wainscotting, he has created in the kitchen a country decor.

Rue des Eperonniers is a small narrow lane with tall, dilapidated houses that lean against each other. The street has a certain medieval atmosphere. The street is very run-down, but Dirk Minet is determined not to give in. He is in fact having his façade and shopfront repainted in the old style. This is not in any way kitsch, but he wants it as it was before. You would swear that this house had been plucked straight from a Parisian street. It should be remembered that 50 years ago Brussels looked just like Paris. Here too, streets were full of well-appointed shopfronts that were profusely painted and bedecked with signs. Many have disappeared, laments Minet, who with his embellished shopfront is showing how things can be done.

IN A CORNER OF PLACE SAINT-JEAN, BEHIND Grand'Place, we encounter the most beautiful shopfront of Brussels. The corner of Rue des Eperonniers shows an old medieval alignment. Formerly there used to be an inn here. Last century the entire district was restyled. Only the shopfront remains as a relic of the past. The shop window and the façade have been painted in an old-fashioned decorative style, for which antique dealer Dirk Minet used an old picture postcard as a model. In the past, too, an elegant lady graced the shopfront. The house seems to have been plucked from a Paris street. Small wonder, for some fifty years ago Brussels strongly resembled the French capital with its elegant shop windows and showy advertisements on the shopfronts. Very few of these charming decorations have been preserved, so it is worth taking some time to admire Dirk Minet's shop. Dirk is very concerned about the appearance of the city and regrets the run-down state of so many districts. 'I am convinced,' he says, 'that the city would look far better if all the people of Brussels would take the trouble to smarten up the fronts of their homes. Then all the ugliness would be far less conspicuous.' He finds it difficult to understand why so many people take pictures of his shop exterior, but do not bother to embellish their own homes. They must like nice buildings, but obviously lack the discipline to do any redecoration themselves.

Dirk has restored his house to its former glory. It used to be a haberdashers but was later turned into a restaurant, when part of the furnishings were removed. The antique cupboards were destroyed. Dirk had replicas made, which he uses to store his collection of old books. Hundreds, perhaps thousands, of these are piled as high as the ceiling. It is impossible to see what colour the walls are, except that over the years they have taken on a yellowish sheen. The shop is very dimly lit, there is just enough light to browse. It almost seems as if the interior is lit by candlelight.

Although Dirk is an experienced and smart trader, he seems more like a collector than a businessman. Collecting books was his first passion. He has been collecting old books for ten years. When he worked in a London hotel his boss was unhappy with him, because he would always be reading or browsing in antique shops. He went the rounds of the London bookshops and always came back with a rucksack full of ancient tomes. As a collector he would only buy first-class editions. Later he went to live in Redu, a book-selling village in the Ardennes, where he opened a bookshop and sold even second-hand penny novels. It was good training, he now says. He gradually improved his business. He now also sells travel books dating from Robinson Crusoe's time and architectural treatises published in the Renaissance. He no longer collects books himself, and now only buys what he can sell in his shop. He compares his wares to vintage wines and is happy to let visitors sample them.

He now concentrates, more than he did in the past, on collecting beautiful objects. These he keeps in his house in Rue du Marché au Charbon. Minet claims that the area where he lives is one of the few remaining authentic neighbourhoods of the city. Nowhere else is the past as tangible. Rue du Marché au Charbon, a long, wide street, used to be the beginning of the trade route to Paris. Pilgrims would walk down the street on their way to Compostela. The street formerly had a chapel-cum-guesthouse, dedicated to St James. Just over three centuries ago this landmark was replaced by a quaint Baroque chapel.

Many pilgrims have passed the door of Minet's shop. Perhaps his shop was once an inn, where weary

travellers dropped in to get drunk. It seems not all that unlikely, for the first-floor room of this narrow house resembles a pub from Teniers' time. Despite its three floors it is one of the smallest houses of Brussels, with a total floor space of less than 30 square metres. 'To me it is like a mill,' says Dirk Minet. The four small rooms are interconnected by an old spiral staircase. Downstairs, almost on the street, is the kitchen. The first floor has a sitting room and the second floor has a small study with a harpsichord. The furnishings are baroque and casual. The slanting planks and lopsided doors and windows have remained just as they were. Dirk even plans to have new windows made that are just as lopsided as the old ones. But he cannot find a carpenter who wants to do the job.

Minet is not originally from Brussels, but he is very much an adopted son of the city. He lives and works hardly a hundred yards from Grand'Place. His house is poignantly simple in its design features. It looks in fact like an old mill, with little rooms arranged around an old spiral staircase. Here in this pied-à-terre on the coal market, even a pilgrim on the way to Compostela would feel at home.

A house full of books and little light. It is
no wonder because most of the volumes
Minet surrounds himself with were penned
by candlelight at a time when electric artificial light was not even dreamed of. Dirk
gets his books just about everywhere, pick-
ing them up from old libraries where time
has no meaning. He is a collector rather
than a businessman and sees his collection
as a good wine cellar where he allows visitors to sample the millésimes.

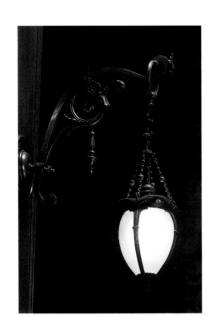

THIS STAIRWELL COULD EASILY ACCOMmodate a three-floor terraced house. If the glass cupola were removed there would be enough room for a roof. It is a large building, with an entrance hall on the second floor. The hall had to be spacious, because it had to accomodate a large chandelier. The original owner was a chandelier manufacturer. The first floor contained workshops and showrooms. Visitors wanting to see the largest chandelier in the collection were invited to go to the hall. All sides of the chandelier could be viewed from the many stairs and galleries. Now that it has gone, the entrance hall is rather like the lobby of a British hunting lodge. The chandelier was sold just before the present owners moved in. I doubt if this should be a cause for regret, for the setting is perfect as it is.

The open layout is reminiscent of Italian Renaissance architecture. Not sixteenth-century Renaissance, but the Neo variety of roughly one hundred years ago. In that Romantic age Neo-Renaissance was very popular in Brabant and Flanders. Many townhouses in Antwerp and Brussels have a hall or dining room designed in this showy style. It was a tribute to the age of Rubens. The abundant wood panelling and the overdecorated wallpaper betray a certain influence from across the Channel. There is a link with traditional English architecture.

The house has been carefully restored. The opulent decorations have been preserved. It is fortunate that this house has never been vacant. Many empty houses have been vandalised in Brussels. Precious furnishings were simply stolen and sold by antique dealers. It is something of a miracle that this house escaped scot-free, because it is situated in a desolate area near the old port, close to Molenbeek. All the more reason to congratulate the new owners with their fine restoration job.

Discovering this house tucked away in a somewhat derelict district close to Molenbeek was a tremendous experience. It is not only an appealing piece of architecture. It is good to know that the property is occupied by a family. The people who live there also know how to use everything, like the central hall, which is the showpiece of this fine residence. We find in this house clear evidence of how much Brussels architects of the past liked to incorporate influences from the north and south of Europe. The hall in Flemish Renaissance style is an ode to the golden age of Antwerp and harks back to the Anglo-Saxon architectural tradition. The influence of Pugin and Morris is never very far away. The house has been tastefully restored, while the original decoration has hardly been touched. Even the imitation gold leather wall covering has been preserved.

When you see this splendidly appointed concrete living space, you might be forgiven for thinking you are in downtown Manhattan rather than in Brussels. The interior designer Axel Verhoustraeten lives in a factory that dates from the 1930s. We can admire his serious and unaffected approach to architecture.

THERE ARE NO FLOWERS TO BE FOUND ON Place du Jardin aux Fleurs, not even a blade of grass or any shrubbery. We are very close to the somewhat desolate community of Molenbeek, once known as the Manchester of the Continent. The neighbourhood off Place du Jardin aux Fleurs is thoroughly industrial in character. Right around the corner is Rue des Fabriques with its many tall concrete buildings set among the houses. But the lack of flowers outside does not bother interior designer Axel Verhoustraeten, because he likes a certain degree of chaos. 'I am a true city dweller,' he states. He does, however, regret the decay and dereliction that Brussels has been prey to in the last few decades. In this working-class neighbourhood he has found intimacy and animation. His house and his workshop are hidden behind the tall buildings lining the square. That is just what he wants, for he feels that this is a time when ostentation is out of place. 'I don't need to publicise my presence,' he says, 'anyone who wishes to look me up, is sure to find me.'

He lives in an unpretentious building with an unfinished façade. It used to be a silver-moulding shop. The building, with its workshop and offices, is strictly functional and was built in a kind of Bauhaus style. At least that is what the tall, metal-framed windows remind us of. The building was finished just a few months before the outbreak of World War II. The previous owner, Jan Vercruysse, an artist, saved the building from decay. He restored it, more or less as Verhoustraeten would have liked it. Verhoustraeten himself hardly carried out any changes at all. He lives in a large room with a light colour scheme. You enter the house via a banistered staircase that seems like a boxing ring. Most surprising is the complete absence of design furniture. This is rather a refreshing touch, for an abundance of design furniture will

be harmful to a house's personality. Verhoustraeten, an interior designer, does not like design furniture because he claims it is dictated too much by fashion.

Axel Verhoustraeten designs his own furniture. Out of necessity, he argues, because he cannot find what he wants in the market. He uses traditional materials like wool and leather, no glass and only rarely metal. His designs have had time to mature, as you can tell by their elaborate shapes. His style is a continuation of pre-war traditions, when the architects Marcel Baugniet and Huib Hoste designed similar furniture.

Almost all the furniture in the apartment was designed by Verhoustraeten, including the huge, four-metre long dinner table. The table seems like a building and is meant to offset the unusually long living room. The furnishings in the library with vases by Allan McCollum are architectural in character and go beyond mere furniture. It is a type of design that has been reflected on at length. These are not computer creations, but furniture that is meant to be an extension of the architecture of a particular room. Verhoustraeten's designs are always tailored to a particular project. Only a few of his pieces of furniture are mass-produced. He has worked for Christian Liaigre among others.

His preference for unique objects also shows in the photographs by Amish Fulton on the walls. This photographer turns very ordinary objects into special treasures. Fulton will wander around in the countryside for seven days and nights, touching stones and taking a single picture of each of them. It is as if after each picture he returns the stone to Mother Nature. His art is almost as volatile and elusive as music. That is precisely what this interior is all about.

The smallest details tell you that Manhattan is never far away. No doubt unconsciously, Verhoustraeten sets about his work of composition rather like a jazz pianist. He creates real musical harmony in the different rhythms we encounter around the house, where individual forms and motifs are repeated everywhere. The best examples are the Allan McCollum vases on the bookshelf.

In a forgotten corner of the dining room, the photographer discovers the part of the house with the purest lines: like a constructivistic sculpture, an ode to the prolific 1930s, when great men like Gropius, Stam and Mondriaan were stripping their work of all contrivance. The staircase is not the creation of a great master but of an unknown architect who was very much in tune with his time. Verhoustraeten preserved the purity of the locus and had Fred Eerdekens inscribe an eloquent phrase.

Is this not a superb setting for a Robert Mangold? The living room has more or less been designed around the work. An enormous wall has been left free for this monumental painting which hangs as the central feature and can be seen from virtually everywhere. The exterior (photograph above) is dominated by Isa Genzken's 'Camera'. This steel frame cuts a slice out of the view of the city.

IN THE OLD HARBOUR DISTRICT OF BRUSSELS, on top of the filled-in docks, near the mysterious Royal Flemish Theatre and the imposing Pacheco Hospital we find the Meert-Rihoux art gallery. The gallery is housed in an old warehouse, dating from the beginning of the century. Behind its simple Art Nouveau front we encounter work by Robert Barry, Donald Judd, Enrico Castellini, Thomas Struth and Isa Genzken. The architects Paul Robbrecht and Hilde Daem were asked to design a pied-à-terre, where artists can stay when their exhibitions are being prepared. The top floor was to be turned into a penthouse with an open kitchen and a large terrace where the occupants would be able to enjoy their surroundings. From the roof a fascinating panorama unfolds. The light-coloured Pacheco building is just below. Beyond, there is the Baroque Beguinage Church. To the North the old town is seen to be gradually swallowed up by towering cranes and skyscrapers. The high-rise buildings are interspersed here and there with derelict townhouses and green areas. Such dramatic views are rare in Belgium. This scarred townscape is both fascinating and heart-rending. It reminds one of New York rather than a medieval town. From up high one also feels the heartbeat of the metropolis, for street noises float up to the fifth floor.

The warehouse is like a pedestal for an architectural still-life. The artist Isa Genzken has been involved in the project from the start. The result can be seen from the street. An immense steel frame of four by five metres leans against the railing of the terrace. The frame protrudes beyond the railing and hovers above the street – a dynamic accent on a static structure. The work is called *Camera*. It cuts out a fragment from the environment. This work of art was already present when Robbrecht and Daem built the

penthouse and was integrated into the three-part still-life. The two remaining parts were crafted by the architects.

They put a tall box on top of the existing structure, creating an enormous sense of space to counteract the overwhelming view. In this way the penthouse got its second floor. The lower part contains a living room, a dining room, a study, a kitchen, a bathroom and two bedrooms. Windows let in the immediate surroundings. The kitchen window cuts out a piece of a mundane high-rise building. From the living room the theatre can be glimpsed. In the dining room the city lies at your feet and you look right across Genzken's camera.

The lower floor has white walls to hang works of art. The large wall was specially designed for a huge picture by Robert Mangold. There are also works by Castellani, Jef Verheyen and Richard Tuttle.

Paul Robbrecht likes to refer to the top floor as a Pandora's box. According to legend this box contained not just disasters, but also a number of pleasant surprises. So it is with the penthouse. On the top floor the city view predominates. Windows have been set in all of the walls, so that the infernal townscape is omnipresent. From the small bathroom and the bedroom a view can be had of the Northern part of Brussels. Anyone who is too sensitive to look at this maimed part of the city can simply pull the curtains shut, turning the penthouse into a closed box. Those who want to immerse themselves in the townscape can step outside onto the metal passageway that serves as a belvedere. The architects feel that the townscape is a work of art that is continuously remodelled. They claim that the building reflects contemporary society, in that it profoundly marks the relation of the individual with the metropolis.

The visitors' room of the Meert-Rihoux art gallery is above a warehouse and can hardly be seen from the street. From here you can see how chaotic the old town is. The former heart of the town is split apart by buildings and cranes. This is beautiful and fascinating but also rather painful. Much is lost, but you will nowhere come across such a spectacular panorama, and certainly not in this country. You feel the throbbing heart of the metropolis. The architects Robbrecht and Daem have opted for an open penthouse that looks out onto the world. In the sedate interior, the emphasis is on the grey painted steel construction that holds the colossal structure together.

Away from
the Beating Heart

IT MAY HAVE BEEN MERE CHANCE, BUT WHEN Belgium had just become independent, the people of Brussels ventured beyond the walls of their city and began to leave its beating heart. Brussels has a heart-shaped layout. The first residents of the Brussels suburbs felt a notch above the rest. In Quartier Leopold they self-assuredly built a modern town, the beating heart of the young nation, with an eye to the future. Money and political power resided in imposing city palaces. This district is now being sacrificed to another transplanted heart, the nearby European quarter. Consequently, Quartier Leopold has lost much of its former attractiveness.

At the time that the gentry created Quartier Leopold, ordinary people, too, began to move out of the city. The workers went north to Molenbeek and the middle-classes settled just about everywhere. They were welcomed by smart property developers, who turned pastures and fields into streets and houses. I suspect that the common people felt rather more heartbroken than the upper ten when they had to leave Brussels. The exterior of their houses seems to confirm this. The Brussels suburbs teem with step-gables and Baroque cornices, modern copies of a remote past. It is as if the people wanted to bring a piece of Grand'Place with them to the suburbs as a souvenir.

But that is only part of the story. The middle-classes built terraced houses with gardens. This was not usual at a time when in Paris, for instance, families crowded together in a single set of rooms. In Brussels two generations would sometimes share a house, together with their servants. Most of the groundplans were rather traditional, with rooms laid out lengthwise. Designers looked to the past for inspiration as far as furnishings were concerned, and the layout of the houses was rather old-fashioned as

well. Many houses that were built roughly a hundred years ago are hardly different in their layout from the medieval houses in the old city centre. Their ground-plans and orientation, with the building set at a right angle to the street, are virtually identical.

This is quite remarkable. This type of architecture is not peculiar to Brussels, for it can be found anywhere in Belgium. Even after World War II many inhabitants of Brussels refused to move into an apartment in a block of flats and continued to build terraced houses. That is why housing in Brussels is quite comfortable. It also means that the city's appearance is completely different from that of most other European cities. The streets in neighbourhoods that haven't been spoilt by new construction seem rather frivolous. There is an immense variety of façades, which is unusual and fascinating. These housefronts reflect the individualistic, stubborn soul of the people. The citizens wanted façades that looked diffferent from their neighbours', whatever the cost. This requirement created much work for architects, decorators, plasterers, marble painters and carpenters. And individualism did not stop with the exterior; the interiors, too, were given a personal touch. All this customised construction and furnishing created a flourishing industry.

The most beautiful creations date from 1860 to 1940. Anyone wandering along the narrow streets of St Giles will agree with me. Consider Rue Vanderschrick, most of which was designed by the architect Eric Blérot. This modest street contains several Art Nouveau treasures. It is unique in Europe. Blérot did not build these houses for rich industrialists, but for ordinary people. Despite the considerable dereliction much has been saved, but finding the most beautiful items requires some effort of exploration. Things are getting better, though, for there is now a

tendency to restore houses rather than demolish them to make place for blocks of flats. The European Community bureaucrats have indirectly helped to bring this about. With their high salaries they have revived the real estate business. Prices are going up and consequently more houses are being preserved. This development is most noticeable in the areas near the ponds of Ixelles and off the imposing Avenue Molière.

Lionel Jadot occupies part of an old townhouse in the run-down neighbourhood behind Gare du Midi. It is a large house with a classical cornice front in Rue Théodore Verhaegen. This street used to be a major artery running across a wealthy district. Unfortunately those days have gone, but Jadot proves that these old houses can be turned into very comfortable homes indeed. The house is set in front of the furniture workshop that he runs with his father. When Jadot moved in, the house had been vacant since the turn of the century. The rooms had been in use as showrooms and had no amenities whatsoever. Refurbishing was carried out with minimal resources.

The large main room is at the north side of Lionel's apartment. It is a kind of art gallery replete with curios. Lionel exhibits all kinds of oddities here. Most conspicuous is a mural on the rear wall, painted by Michel Strijkers and strikingly similar to an antique fresco. Two chandeliers hang from the ceiling. One, a solid wrought-iron artifice, decorated with dragons holding oil lamps, comes from an Italian country home. It has a threatening rather than a frivolous aspect. And it is a bit kitschy, but that goes with the rest of the interior. Of course, the room is full of chairs, which were found in the attics over the workshop. Some of them may have been made by Vanhamme, who founded the chair manufactory in

This is an interior created by a young collector who has grown up among antique furniture. He dwells here in a spacious flat behind a stately façade in the tumultuous Rue Verhaegen, close to the Gare du Midi. The large living room on the north side is crammed with the fruits of his serendipity. Here he puts on show the strangest objects. There is a touch of crazy and droll kitsch in certain features like the chandelier with the dragon motifs.

83

1870, when the Napoleon III style was popular and everyone wanted plush furniture. The funniest piece of furniture in the room stands just below the other chandelier – it is a large easy chair with legs in the shape of animals. Because it is slightly lopsided, it seems like a kind of pony. Our host thinks it is an English chair, made for the Indian market. Lionel uses an old-fashioned tabouret for a coffee-table. But he is not really a collector of chairs. His apartment contains very few genuinely antique chairs. Most are 150 years old at best.

The large north room is not really used as a living room. It serves as a passage to the kitchen, which is hidden away in a corner. Lionel had it built in a kind of niche. He did not want an ordinary kitchen and had a small roof constructed on the ceiling. He covered the wall with old doors – cheap panelling. The result is a cooking place that resembles a beach house.

Adjacent to the exhibit room is a small, cosy sitting room where heavy curtains keep the sunlight out. The decorations, including paper masks on the wall, are a tribute to Ensor. The mantelpiece holds a collection of bric-a-brac, odd bits and pieces bought randomly by Lionel.

His most precious ornament is in the entrance hall – a children's chair his father gave him. Another door leads to the bedroom with a four-poster bed – made by Lionel himself – and two *trompe l'oeil* windows by Strijkers. The room contains a surprising amount of church furniture.

Even though Jadot designs modern mass-produced furniture he does not want a contemporary interior. He feels such interiors lack the spontaneity of old trashy objects.

At the rear of the house is the bathroom, with a sunken tub and opening onto a nice terrace. This

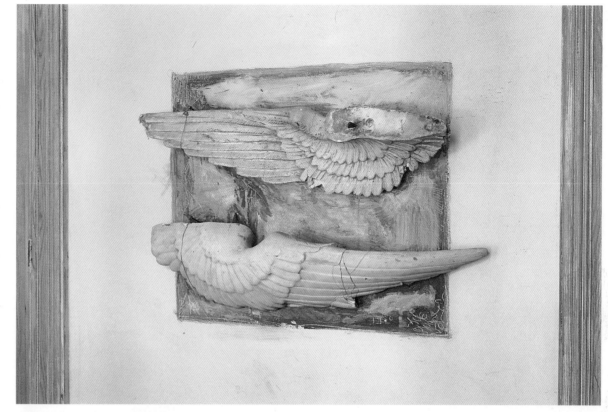

Evidently, this interior is just too bourgeois in style for Lionel Jadot! He just cannot take the architecture seriously. This can certainly be said for the sitting room on the garden side. The fireplace is full of knick-knacks that he has picked up in junk shops. Nothing outlandishly expensive here! This is exactly what he wanted: decoration with a sense of humour and a note of surrealism. Just take a look at the church furniture. He will stop at nothing to contrast starkness and ostentatious refinement.

tiny roof garden seems larger than it actually is, because there are a lot of easy chairs, flower pots and old stones. In summer it is used as a living room. The ochre walls make one think of Provence rather than the centre of Brussels. If you think away the roofs outside and replace them in your imagination by cypresses you seem to be in the South of France.

From the outside, Christophe Decarpentrie's house is reminiscent of a school in a French colony: a simple concrete construction with harmonious proportions. Inside, however, you are suddenly struck by a riot of styles, colours and smells. In the small vestibule with its neo-Gothic decor, you come across the sacred odour of incense, while in the delightful living room you are assailed by the smell of cooking herbs from the garden.

DESIGNER CHRISTOPHE DECARPENTRIE IS a keen talker, who will tell you all about European history while showing you around his house. He has a tendency to see connections between everything and will relate the most disparate cultures to each other. His analysis of Flemish popular culture involves the Romans, the Germanic peoples and the Celts. This wide-ranging approach is also apparent in the furnishings of his house, which display a mixture of styles and atmospheres, ranging from Louis Quinze to William Morris. 'Eclecticism,' he once told me, 'is the strong point of the Belgians. The Dutch, French and Germans are too single-minded for it, they cannot switch from one style to another. But we are less inclined to stick to one particular style. Belgians can thoroughly enjoy a cantata by Bach one moment and join in a pub dance the next.' He is right. The streets of Brussels are the best example of this unchecked chaos of styles.

Decarpentrie's interior is like one of those streets with highly different façades. The living room, actually a large entrance hall, is teeming with seating areas. It contains an improbable number of chairs and couches, as if everything has been got ready for a big party. And yet, there is unity in this chaos, thanks to the building itself. One glance at the heavy beams of the ceiling will make this clear. They help to fuse the furnishings into a whole, an effect that is further helped along by the glass panel designed by Decarpentrie's partner Abel Naessens and separating one of the seating areas from the dining area. The stark, austere architecture enhances the atmosphere.

It is an odd building, whose exterior looks like a French colonial school. The abundant greenery in the garden and the ochre walls create an additional mediterranean touch. But the building has never been a school, although it has been used as a card-players' club, a library, a gymnasium and even a cinema. The movie theatre on the second floor has been preserved in its original state, including the proscenium. Here Decarpentrie stores furniture and antique objects.

The house dates from 1903 and was built on the site of a former chapel. 'When digging in the garden we found traces of the medieval chapel,' Christophe Decarpentrie proudly reports. His pride is understandable, for he is a keen historian. He can tell you about the origin and age of every object in his home. Some of his possessions are absolutely unique. At a very early age he began collecting neo-Gothic objects. This style became quite prominent in Belgium, especially in Flanders, where the rediscovery of the Middle Ages was encouraged by the British Gothic revival of a century and a half ago. The showpiece of Decarpentrie's collection is a magnificent rosewood easy chair, designed by Viollet-le-Duc. The same room contains a chair by William Morris and two chairs that once belonged to Sir Lawrence Alma-Tadema, the Dutchman whose mock-antique paintings became all the rage in England. Few people know that in the 1860s Tadema took lessons at the Antwerp art college, then an establishment of international repute. Later he moved to Brussels, where he became friends with Joseph Poelaert, the architect of the Palais de Justice. The Romanesque chairs date from his Brussels period.

Decarpentrie has devoted an entire room to his neo-Gothic collection, furnishing it with dark blue wallpaper covered with gilt lilies as a tribute to the French royal dynasty.

He likes surrealistic touches. It shows in the whimsical furniture and the chandeliers made of antlers.

And there are still other unusual objects. The walls are singularly lacking in mirrors or paintings. Most frames are standing on the floor. 'I have several reasons for this,' he states. 'For one thing, I saw it in Vermeer. He sometimes hangs frames above eye-level. I feel that walls should be empty, creating areas of rest. Besides, I like putting things down on the floor. It is part of my nomadic nature, I need to feel that I can move out any minute.'

A theatre decor with the pomp and splendour of a bygone era. This interior features antique Venetian cabriolet seats and Spanish chairs dating from the time of Rubens. Christophe Decarpentrie is certainly a lover of the frivolities of Baroque.

It is hard to imagine that this building is in the centre of the city, tucked away behind rows of terraced houses and far from the hustle and bustle.

The structure of the property is perfect, with lots of windows and doors on the side overlooking the garden. The architecture is not even a century old, but it already has a rich history. Indeed, the property contains the remains of a medieval chapel.

ALTHOUGH THIERY BOUTEMY SETTLED IN a small working-class house in a Brussels slum, he hails from Normandy. On the spot where Chaussée d'Alsemberg enters the working-class areas of Forest, Boutemy runs a flower shop below a convivial restaurant called Le pain et le vin. The small shop, with its low ceilings and dark walls, is like a cave. Boutemy is a very relaxed person and with his long black hair looks like a Red Indian. But his roots are not in America. Just a few years ago he still lived in his native region near Mont-Saint-Michel. Five years ago he arrived in Leuven, where he got a job with Amadeus, the famous flower shop. He had escaped from Honfleu, a beuatiful little town, where life was too dull for his taste. Paris, on the other hand, was too busy to appeal to him. Eventually he ended up in Brussels, where he opened a small flower shop, hoping to breathe new life into the rather derelict neighbourhood. He found a small house in a narrow alley behind Chaussée d'Alsemberg. The alley is like a small island in the city, where all kinds of people feel at home. His neighbours include a doctor, a conductor and an antique dealer, as well as more ordinary people, who grow vegetables and breed chickens in their small gardens. He truly feels at home here, in this mixed urban and rural environment. 'I have always remained a countryman at heart,' he explains, 'and I need a green environment. In Paris such neighbourhoods are extremely rare, and where they can be found they are very posh and expensive. I don't feel at ease there. Brussels is far less uptight than the French capital. The people, too, are less ostentatious. But I miss the French countryside and especially that of Normandy, where far less damage has been done than in Belgium. So much has been spoilt here. It's a great shame.'

Boutemy's house is older than you may think. It was built at the time of the construction of the Palais de Justice, in the 1860s. Joseph Poelaert, the architect, built a series of cottages to house his workers. They are very small, with a floor space of less than 10 square metres. Boutemy's home consists of three rooms on top of each other. Even the mantelpieces are tiny. Yet the house is full of interesting bric-a-brac. Some of the furniture is rather baroque, such as the massive tabernacle by the window.

Before Boutemy moved in, the house was thoroughly cleaned and repainted. But there are few luxuries. Boutemy does not even have a telephone or a TV set and he does not want a radio, for, as he says, all you ever hear on the news are horrible disasters.

In his quest for peace and quiet he offers nature a place in his home in the shape of coulourful bouquets. The interior is a reminder of the countryside – the colour scheme ranges from brown to green, and the materials include wood, straw, earthenware and wicker. Boutemy is something of an explorer and he likes oddities. He discovered the strange tabernacle in a junkyard. This monstrosity is more than two hundred years old. I should never dare to put it in such a small space, but here it does not clash with the many other curios that fill the room. Straw figures hang from the ceiling near the tabernacle. These are simple examples of local folk art. They are lucky charms made by an elderly lady from the Tournai region.

Because the dining room is so small, Boutemy put the table against the wall like a console. The globes on the cupboard, the lamb and the flowers made of gilt wire are also specimens of genuine folk art. Boutemy is fond of antique home-made objects and thinks they are much more charming and genuine than expensive objects of art.

Thierry Boutemy has a keen nose and is blessed with serendipity everywhere he goes. A scrap merchant set him on the trail of this tabernacle. The straw figures that hang next to it are examples of authentic folk art from the Belgian hinterland. They are in fact lucky charms fashioned by an elderly lady from near Tournai.

The furnishings in his home are more than just decorations.

Boutemy has created a true *trompe-l'oeil*. The house is tiny and lacked any kind of style or embellishment. But now the furnishings take you along on a journey. Downstairs everything is distinctly French and rural. Upstairs there is a Gustavian bedroom with grey walls and light furniture.

The small kitchen was only recently furnished. There is hardly room to cook and yet Boutemy has filled this room with things he found in the fleamarket. Every week he goes browsing in the fleamarket on Place du Jeu de Balle. He can be found there every Thursday morning at five-thirty.

94

You would not think it possible to find a kitchen in which there is barely enough room to cook or eat. However, it is certainly worthwhile to take a look at all the things that Thierry Boutemy has collected in less than no time. But the bedroom, with its Gustavian decor, is quite different. Here white, grey and touches of gold paint dominate. The richness is only thinly disguised, but it is not evident in the dimensions (after all, the bedrooms only measure a few square metres) or in the luxury. Even the radio and the telephone have been banished from this house.

Antique dealer Alic and his wife Sophie are certainly more fond of 'la France Profonde' than of Brussels. This can clearly be seen from the serenity of their interior. They spend much of the year in the Poitou, where they have done up an old farmhouse and spent some time looking around for objets d'art for their shop. Alic has a small cabinet where he keeps other souvenirs from Africa, where he once lived.

THE WAY ALIC SHOWS YOU AROUND HIS shop betrays that he is a collector. His hands caress every object he shows you. He is not the type of collector who concentrates on a single type of object. He is interested in anything that used to be found on farms. Alic, a designer, has lost his heart to 'la France profonde'. He and his wife Sophie are restoring an old country house in Poitou, which has been uninhabited since times immemorial. On his travels in the Poitou region he looks for suitable objects to sell in L'Authentique, his Brussels shop. The shop is not cluttered, for Alic likes bare walls, painted in pale earth colours. The collection on show in L'Authentique would do credit to a folklore museum. Damaged earthenware dishes, stoneware jars and wicker breadbaskets are ranged on old kitchen tables. These objects are hardly decorated at all, but they do show signs of wear and tear. That doesn't bother Alic, on the contrary.

His house exudes a peaceful atmosphere, which is unusual in the centre of Brussels. He lives near the La Cambre Abbey on the banks of one of the Ixelles ponds in a distinguished terraced house with interlinking rooms. The groundplan is quite common, unlike the atmosphere. Only the first-floor sitting room has a somewhat bourgeois character because of the marble mantelpiece and the stucco decorations. On a tour of the house it becomes clear that its personality is revealed in details. On the mantel are antique earthenware saucers and an ointment pot found during an archeological dig. There is a worn statue as well, found in a burnt chapel. Alic made the coffee-table from an iron sheet he found in a deserted coalmine.

The dining room adjacent to the garden is almost abstract in its conception. The walls and furniture were painted in light shades. The only touch of bright colour is a bottle of red wine. This simplicity is needed in order not to draw attention away from the objects in the room. Souvenirs are displayed on top of a cupboard – a tin plate, a coat of arms from Zaire and a handful of other bibelots.

The second-floor room is less austere, but even more beautiful. It is a masculine room full of mementoes. The large display cabinet contains a wealth of memories. This is where Alic keeps his wicker-covered bottles. There are also a pair of compasses, a toy giraffe, small mirrors and some highly unusual boxes. Many objects are reminiscent of Congo, the former colony where he was born and grew up. Perhaps this is why he admires simple utensils, the sort of things that used to be thrown away after use. And perhaps this also explains his love for France, a country where delapidated houses tend to be restored rather than pulled down and where worm-eaten cupboards are not burnt but restored without hiding signs of wear and tear. A different approach to what we are used to, especially in Brussels and Flanders, where worn objects are either thrown away or restored to pristine condition. Antique dealers are aware of this: mended dishes are hard to sell in this country and lose all their value.

Sophie and Alic find it a pity that things that are worn are destroyed, so they have affection for these discarded trouvailles. This kitchen cabinet in the study does not contain costly trinkets but rather old utensils that have thoughtlessly been thrown away.

It must be delightful to work in this room. It is just brimming with inspiration because every object has its own story to tell. Look, for example, at the massive wine-bottle rack in the foreground – a real sculpture. Alic shows his hand here. After all, he once worked as a fashion photographer and portraitist. This explains the orderly arrangement of all these beautiful objects.

Decorating is basically learning to sit down and look at things. In contemporary interiors, objects appear that previously no-one would have paid any attention to. There is a kind of subtle poetry in such objects. Just take for example this broken pan or the weathered old padlock. They are so charming that you just cannot throw them away. These seemingly useless objects have been collected by Alic. They are in fact quite touching, because they come from simple country folk.

This is a still life decor to which a bottle of wine adds the only splash of colour. The rest of this interior is serene, fragile and empty. The table and chairs come from an ordinary kitchen. The cage is not the showpiece but has definite persuasive power. This is where the daily meal is taken. What a difference in atmosphere compared with the street on which this house stands, with its bourgeois houses in the French style, full of decorative pomp and ostentation.

Place de Londres has escaped the attention of the property developers who have set to Brussels with their demolition hammer. This is all the more surprising as it is close to the European district. But Martine Doly certainly is not complaining as she has picked up this old piece of property with a house overlooking the street, its interior garden and a workshop. She spends her time in all the different corners of the house. The main dining room (above) is next to the kitchen, on the street side. From the kitchen (right), the interior window overlooks the entrance hall where there is nothing to see but a bench.

IT IS DEFINITELY A STROKE OF BAD LUCK IF you restore an old building, which then soon afterwards burns down. It requires a lot of courage and determination to start all over again. Especially if the fire turns out to be not the only setback. During restoration the rear façade came loose from the rest of the building, which very nearly collapsed like a house of cards. 'In spite of everything we are very happy to live here,' says Martine Doly. 'We're just a stone's throw from the city centre. We can get wherever we like on foot or by bike. When we were still living in the countryside we were stuck for hours in traffic jams every day. And during weekends it is actually quieter here than it is in the countryside!' Doly's house is situated off Place de Londres, in a neighbourhood that has not yet been discovered by trendsetters. The headquarters of the European Community are nearby and the king lives just round the corner. A short distance towards Avenue Louise will take us to the lively African district of Brussels. In summertime the people there live out in the streets and will often organise lively street-parties. The area around Place de Londres has retained some of its original intimacy. Pubs and grocery shops are plentiful and there is an auction hall as well. Real estate is far cheaper here than in the centre of Ixelles or Uccle, allowing young people to buy large houses at a reasonable price. But they have to be prepared to do a lot of hard work. Many houses are derelict so that restoration takes a good deal of energy and money. The effort is worth it, for there are many beautiful houses off Place de Londres. Most of them were built before 1850 in an unostentatious Neo-classical style. Their proportions are similar to seventeenth-century houses. Many of them contain workshops. Old carriage gates hide passages and courtyards.

This building is full of surprises as well. The front part of the house on the street side probably contained offices. Now it has a kitchen, a dining room and bedrooms. Beyond the courtyard is another building, which was formerly a workshop with living quarters. No-one knows what used to be manufactured or stored here. The rear building with its mansard roof would not be out of place in the heart of the Marais district of Paris. The rear façades have been repainted in a soft sandstone colour, very common in France. The front and rear of the house are connected by a covered porch.

Martine Doly's house is large. But then, she needs a lot of space for her family and for the workshop where she and her husband design household linen. Martine has a magnificent linen shop on Boulevard de Waterloo whose modern interior design draws much attention. It was in fact the reason why we visited her at home. Doly tries to ignore fashions in her linen designs: 'My linen should last for a long time. What annoys me about fashion and design is that trends are so ephemeral and become obsolete so fast. That may be the reason why I have quite a lot of old things in my home.' The furnishings of her house are contemporary but not fashionably modern, as is evident from the sanded wooden floors and the walls that have been subtly distempered.

Martine strongly values craftsmanship and reliable materials. 'That is not really all that usual,' she says, 'for there is a lot of poor finishing in construction. Just think of the horrible metal and plastic windowframes that are now generally in use. It is difficult to find beautiful materials and these days you will have to really urge craftsmen to give a beautiful finish to windows, for instance. Most carpenters prefer to take the easy way out and will use standard sizes. They respect their own skills less and less.'

This is the atelier where Martine and her husband design their collection of house-hold linens. Strange... there is nothing that might suggest any such activity. Perhaps it is planned that way, as this room is an artist's workshop.
The collection flies in the face of current trends. This is a conscious decision, as it disturbs Martine to think that fashion and interiors change so quickly. She likes things that last, so you will not find any designer furniture here.

This is the living room at the back of the house. The concrete ceiling reveals that this was formerly a workshop and storage facility. The staircase creates a fascinating visual effect. The decor is not by any means an ode to Europe, as the objects come from just about everywhere. They include textiles from Cuba and the Congo and an enormous vase from Oceania.

Martine Doly attaches great importance to craftsmanship and regrets that much construction work is poorly finished. Attractive properties are cheapened by the use of low-quality materials such as plastic. Here, everything has been carefully restored despite the considerable damage caused to the house by a fire.

This house certainly does not need sunshine and blue skies to suggest a Mediterranean atmosphere as this is all too evident in the contrast between the white interior and the deep red façade. Architect Marc Corbiau and interior designer Jean De Meulder have achieved perfect symbiosis. The high ceilings and the many vertical lines created by the alcoves and windows reinforce the effect of the low furniture.

ARC CORBIAU IS BELGIUM'S MOST mediterranean architect. His inspiration comes from ancient mediterranean models. His designs are based on the villas built by Palladio, the architect from Vicenza who drew on examples from Antiquity. This villa in Uccle is an excellent illustration of Corbiau's work. The symmetrically laid-out house with its wide, sun-oriented groundplan is a true summer residence. Even the red colour of the front hints at Southern regions. Such details may not be essential, but the groundplan is. Consider for instance the plan of Palladio's Villa Thiene, a building designed with bold lines whose focus is a central hall, with a spacious sitting room giving out on the garden behind it. Jacques-François Blondel used similar layouts. Around the central unit Blondel would design a *Salle de Compagnie*, consisting of a number of rooms where people could take a nap and where guests could be received.

Corbiau's design resembles that of his predecessors. Of course, the layout was adapted to a contemporary lifestyle. The house is much more compact than its models, because formerly the sitting-rooms had to be strictly separated from the servants' quarters. The large sitting-room on the garden side is the main room of the house. To its right is a dining-room, to its left a library. The sitting-room is a kind of hall with a high ceiling. Niches in the walls provide vistas. Looking down from the gallery in the living room you will catch a glimpse of the dining table and the grass covering the side of the house.

With this design Corbiau has gone off on a tangent, since most of his colleagues tend to experiment with the construction and function of the rooms of a house.

It is striking how well the architect and the interior designer, Jean De Meulder, have complemented

each other. This was by no means their first joint project. De Meulder has perfectly understood the function of the large sitting-room. Unconsciously he has used an eighteenth-century approach to the furnishings. He created three seating areas along the walls, leaving enough room in the centre for people to circulate. Most of the furniture is contemporary, but De Meulder does not hesitate to use antique furniture as well. Not truly ancient pieces, of course, but furniture that was modern at the beginning of the century. He is particularly fond of that period and his own home contains furniture by Adolf Loos and Marcel Kammerer. This interior contains an Arts and Crafts easy chair. It is not a replica, of course, for De Mulder will only use original pieces.

This flat is set in the reception wing of a spacious mansion dating from the Belle Epoque. This can still be seen from the stucco that embellishes the ceiling. It is an enormous room, almost like a hall, where Eline De Potter has found enough space to build a mezzanine which she uses as a bedroom. The flat is compact but airy. The decoration is somewhat reminiscent of the Roaring Twenties. Eline has decorated the interior with a touch of humour. For example, take a look at the Fornasetti dishes beside the dining table. The kitchen is a cabinet full of souvenirs from journeys to far-flung places.

I N RUE DARWIN I LOOKED IN VAIN FOR A sign of the Galapagos Islands. Though this street is full of townhouses with richly ornamented façades no architect was apparently ever seized by the idea to devote a bit of sculpture to this remarkable archipelago in the Pacific. Odd, for an Art Nouveau front with a large tile tableau of an iguana or a giant turtle would look rather nice. Only at Eline De Potter's did I encounter a minor reference to Darwin. She has put two funny plastic cactuses in her window. She has a small collection of perfume bottles decorated with cactuses and designed by Hilton Mac Connico for Daum. It may not be much of a reference to Darwin, but at least it is better than nothing. She claims that some of the people living in the street never even heard of Darwin. Just imagine.

You can be sure that the name of the street was Eline's main motivation to go and live here. She also likes the beautiful neihbourhood with its many magnificent houses. As she lives in the centre of the city she doesn't need a car. The area is teeming with shops, restaurants and antique dealers.

Her apartment would really be more appropriate in Paris. By Brussels standards it is rather small, whereas in the French capital single-room apartments are quite common. But Eline has furnished her apartment with such ingenuity that it seems much larger than it really is. She lives in the reception room of a *Belle Epoque* mansion. It is in fact a small hall with a four-metre high ceiling. It is spacious enough to have room for a mezzanine that is used as a bedroom. The decorations are reminiscent of the Paris of the Roaring Twenties. The colour scheme, the furniture and the bric-a-brac all hint at the interwar years. She has hung some beautiful portraits on the walls, including a flamboyantly drawn pastel of her grandmother.

THE NOBLE NAME OF ISABELLE DE BORCH-grave takes you back to a past of country homes and castles. But I find it difficult to associate her with castles, because her style of decoration is not at all medieval. Her artistic roots go back to the era of the painter and architect Charles le Brun, who created the *Manufacture Royale des Meubles de la Couronne* for Louis XV. This huge manufactory provided the French king's palaces with furniture, tapestries, sculpture, silverware and other furnishings. Isabelle de Borchgrave would have felt at home in the Manufacture; she too is highly versatile. She designs tapestries with as much flair as she does tableware.

Isabelle de Borchgrave is not only known in Paris and London, but she also has a solid reputation in New York. Her career began in the seventies with the opening of her boutique La Tour de Bebelle. First she designed printed materials but her activities have meanwhile been expanded to include every single aspect of interior design. She now designs tableware, wallpaper, carpets and tiles. Her workshop also produces murals and garden ornaments. Her creativity covers many fields, much like le Brun's Manufacture. There is also a stylistic relationship. Isabelle de Borchgrave's dynamism is reflected in her love of lively settings with an abundance of flamboyant ornaments. Like Berain and Marot de Borchgrave suffers from horror vacui – she prefers arabesques in rich colours to vacant spaces and bland colours. Isabelle de Borchgrave fits perfectly in Brussels. She lives and works behind Avenue Louise in a neighbourhood of *Belle Epoque* houses, full of wrought-iron and stone ornaments.

A hundred years ago interior decorator Isabelle de Borchgrave would have earned her reputation as a designer of theatre buildings or coffee houses. Her theatrical style is in fact better suited to that bygone era when such opulence was appreciated. Her own house is the most telling and beautiful evidence of this. She has refurbished this property dating from the end of the last century in a playful and frivolous manner.

JAMES ENSOR WOULD HAVE LIKED THIS APARTment, for it is very similar to the interior of his house in Ostend. It has the same odd mixture of souvenirs and ornaments. Ensor owned just such a grotto armchair, like a one-piece shell sculpture. Ensor loved shells, of course, having grown up among them. His parents had a novelty shop where they sold postcards, shells and dried sea monsters. The celebrated artist's attention would certainly have been drawn by the golden étagère set against the dark wall. This fine piece of furniture is packed with precious shells made of china, glass or silver.

Ensor would have felt even more strongly attracted to the screen separating the seating area from the bedroom. It is a curio from the era of Napoleon III, the dictator who flourished at the time of Ensor's youth. At that time interior design was plunged into a dark bath – black was the fashionable colour. The screen is beautiful and very fragile. It is a miracle that it has survived at all. The owner, a well-known Brussels antique dealer with a sixth sense for oddities, has done something weird to it. She has hung a picture of wild flowers on it. The picture is by Lucie

Utrillo, the famous painter's wife, who began her career in the fifties. Ensor would not have considerd the combination beautiful, but he would have been amused by the odd contrast. The tableau would certainly have brought a smile to his lips.

Ensor would especially have appreciated the liveliness of the furnishings. By present-day standards they are rather overpowering. That is a conscious choice. The apartment is part of a mundane post-war block of flats. This rather suited the occupant. It meant that she did not have to be respectful of anything and could furnish her interior just as she liked it. She has accomplished this with a good deal of ingenuity. The seating area and the bedroom of this tiny flat are interlinked, with only some furniture to separate them. The decorations are a mixture of curios. The bedroom is a tribute to the twenties; in one corner is a cubistic painting by Tamara de Lempicka. Everyone thinks it is genuine, but in fact it is a copy, hung here to enliven the interior. A refreshing touch was required to offset all the ninteenth-century objects. The painting provides a light shock. Ensor would have understood perfectly.

Nothing has been left to chance here. Every object is the fruit of long, painstaking research at antique dealers and in old mansions full of long-forgotten keepsakes. Nothing is contemporary because – you must admit – where else can you find so many authentic antique grotto armchairs and such fine embroidery from before the French Revolution? The many flounces certainly add extravagance but are never tedious.

Close to the heart of the African district of Brussels, on the third floor of a building, we find the diminutive flat occupied by antique dealer Christian de Meeüs. This is indeed a strange place to find a man with such an exceptional sensitivity for the past. He is crazy about old art, but he does not like overstated extravagance. Christian de Meeüs has an eye for eighteenth century antiques which – to his chagrin – are becoming increasingly rare.

CHRISTIAN DE MEEÜS, AN ANTIQUE dealer, commutes between Sablon and the African quarter near Porte de Namur. His shop and his house are inconspicuously situated in a side street, which is probably just as he likes it. He lives in a small apartment in a tall house. His apartment consists of a set of former servant's rooms. Their simplicity is not a handicap, because his interior is not classical. But it is not modern either, for none of the furnishings are contemporary. And yet it is an up-to-date interior, because it has been conceptualised as a painting. Fate helped in the matter. Underneath the wallpaper Christian de Meeüs discovered the original paint in beautiful colours. The colour scheme was enhanced by the ravages of time. His deorations have a touch of surrealism, including as they do funny candlesticks, plaster masks and other bric-a-brac. There are no precious objects, only unusual curios. de Meeüs feels that very expensive objects are not necessarily beautiful. He is right, for opulent eighteenth-century showpieces, like furniture covered with bronze fixtures and marquetry, is often too showy. That is not to his taste. He does not even require expensive materials and is quite happy with painted tin, stucco ornaments or simply painted wood. But he wants things to look charming. He is particularly fond of eighteenth-century antiquities, which he sells in his shop. He says that really good objects are increasingly difficult to find. Some decades ago the supply of good antiques was much larger than now. 'We antique dealers', he says, 'are dependent on stocks that are almost exhausted. You may compare it to a shoeshop where the most beautiful shoes are only available in a few unusual sizes. The problem is that reordering is impossible, because there are no manufacturers anymore.'

SINCE VIOLAINE DAMIEN BEGAN TRAVELLING her life has undergone a transformation. She found a new job and threw out half her furniture. Now she travels from Senegal to India and brings back souvenirs from all over the world. In the stairwell of her modest terraced house hang glass paintings from Senegal as well as yellowed portraits of elderly maharajas. Violaine is always on the lookout for interesting mementoes, but she deliberately does not look for really precious objects. She simply tries to find things that ordinary people use in their homes, ranging from tin kitchen utensils from Rajastan to preservers from Morocco. What she cannot use in her own home she sells in her shop. Violaine also tries to find curios in Brussels. In the fleamarket she has found paintings of ships, for instance. The entrance hall of her house now contains many tall framed prints of mailboats. She is fascinated by the sea, even though she was born far inland. Violaine grew up in the rural region of Tournai. Her most impressive find she put in the living room – flanking the mantelpiece are two large iron crosses that once graced the funnels of an ocean-going ship. It is an impressive touch.

Although Violaine Damien was raised in the rural district of Tournai, she is very keen on ocean-going ships. Her house is in fact full of pictures of ships that she picked up at fleamarkets. However, her show-pieces hang in the sitting room on the first floor. Next to the fireplace on rough, badly-damaged walls she has hung two iron crosses that once graced the funnels of a mailboat.

THIS HOUSE IS FULL OF THE MEMORIES of youth, whispers Roland Gerard when showing me his kitchen. There is barely enough room for the two of us and the light is rather dim, too. 'It reminds me of the kitchen in my parents' home,' he continues, 'where I used to play as a child when my mother was cooking. It was warm and smelled lovely. I feel that smell should penetrate the entire house. It makes the kitchen more beautiful as well, for all the juices season the wood and create living colours.' It is hard to imagine that the kitchen is a recent creation. Roland has made almost everything himself, including the cupboards. He has selected each piece of wood himself. He could hardly have commisssioned someone else to design such a log-cabin kitchen, since no carpenter would have understood his intentions. He has used highly unusual building materials, such as moldering tree trunks and pieces of parquetry that he stuck upside down on the ceiling. It is an approach that requires some imagination. He has used square wooden plaquettes rather than tiles to cover the wall behind the sink. The sink itself is simply an antique stone basin. The kitchen seems very simple indeed. The materials are simple, straightforward and rural. A piece of zinc has been put on top of a cupboard. There are hardly any modern amenities. The equipment is limited to the bare essentials. That is just how Roland's wife Marie-Rose, who uses the kitchen intensively, likes it. She prefers to use old-fashioned utensils when cooking. The cupboards are full of cast-iron pots, earthenware dishes and old-fashioned tin baking moulds. This house on the edge of Forêt de Soignes is like a hermitage, a refuge that the modern age has passed by. Time seems to have a different quality here, for nowhere else does the clock tick quite so slowly.

Old workshops and warehouses lend themselves to the type of thorough conversion work whereby they end up looking like an ordinary house. However, in the process, all the industrial period is lost. Here, the architects de Liedekerke and Ketelbuters have given free rein to their imagination and exploited certain features of the factory architecture.

In the middle of this space they have placed a mezzanine with unadorned metal-framed windows. The view from up there is quite a surprise. Because the building is situated in a posh district (on Place du Châtelain in St Giles), this unassuming loft is all the more attractive. However, it is not an ordinary house, and with just a few touches here and there it could once again become a workshop.

THIS LOFT IS SITUATED OFF PLACE DU Châtelain in St Giles in a quiet bourgeois district with imposing houses. Here and there we encounter striking façades, such as the one of Horta's home. It is a convivial neighbourhood to live in and to visit. There are amusing little shops and each Wednesday the square is the scene of a picturesque street market, where Italian rather than French or Flemish is spoken. You won't find factory buildings here, but there are depots and workshops. This loft is part of such a building. The architects Nicolas de Liedekerke and Stany Ketelbuters have ingeniously restyled their home by constructing a central mezzanine. It is not an entresol with an open gallery, but a closed structure with simple iron-framed windows. Simple, elegant and appropriate to the building. This extra floor has a diagonal layout – unusual, but functional, as the design creates more room. The mezzanine is contemporary in conception, but it does not clash with the sturdy brick build-ing. The many windows and interior walls create very intimate antechambers and make the groundplan rather surprising. Thus it is possible to peep into the bedroom from the bathroom or to glimpse the dining table. The layout goes very well with the architecture. The loft has kept a certain industrial character. The designers therefore decided not to use precious materials. The mezzanine reminds us in a sense of an old-fashioned office from where the boss could keep an eye on his staff. This loft is a very pleasant and spacious home with a large terrace to boot.

Between Dream and Reality

IN ORDER TO DISCOVER THE DEEPEST ROOTS of Art Nouveau you will have to visit the triangle formed by Avenue Louise, Chaussée de Charleroi and Avenue Molière. This elegant neighbourhood has escaped more or less unscathed from the frenetic demolition of the last decades. In this quiet district you can still quietly admire the beautiful façades. It has always been a distinguished neighbourhood for the gentry and the aristocracy, for bankers and industrialists. Their tall, imposing houses commanded respect among the hoi polloi living in the other districts of St Giles. Even now the architecture has an impressive effect on passers-by. During weekends many people interested in architecture visit the neighbourhood in search of Art Nouveau landmarks, of which there are many. Over a period of just a few years, from 1893 to 1900, famous architects like Victor Horta, Henry Van de Velde and Octave Van Rysselberghe built houses that influenced architecture until far into the twentieth century. They determined the appearance of Brussels. Before they started their work façades used to be monotonously Neo-classical, set with intricate cornices, tall friezes and small balconies. The groundplans were just as predictable, with neatly interlinking rooms.

The young architects were fed up with such 'dull' houses. Their quest for new designs was encouraged by the revolutionary spirit of the age that changed literature, music and painting. Remember that Brussels in the 1880s played a major part in modern sculpture. Thanks to the cultural association of Le Groupe des XX, whose members included Khnopff, Ensor, Van de Velde, Toorop and Rodin, exhibitions and concerts of international significance took place. Exhibitions of works by Whistler, Van Gogh, Seurat and Monet were held. In the 1890s the pioneering role of Les Vingts was continued by the group La

Victor Horta, Henry Van de Velde and Octave Van Rysselberghe endowed Brussels with a number of milestones in the history of Art Noveau architecture. Their genius was supported by the talent and interest of many artists, artisans, intellectuals and industrialists. Their avant-garde art appealed to a surprisingly large public. Why was this? After the period of banal historism, there was a call for renewal. The break with the past was more abrupt than we now imagine. A case in point is the living room in the Victor Horta house where nothing remains that is in any way reminiscent of the past.

123

two houses. His own house from 1912 is less modern than the large house he built in 1894 for Paul Otlet. Here, too, bow windows are set in an asymmetrical façade. Henry Van de Velde designed the interior. In the next street is Van Rysselberghe's oldest creation, the house of Count d'Alviella. Despite its basic Neoclassical design the house, from 1882, is progressive in the structuring of its façade and its sgraffito murals.

The most mysterious façade of Brussels is no doubt the house built for the artist Albert Ciambelani in Rue Defacqz, designed by Paul Hankar. The tall curtain wall seems medieval. No wonder, for Ciambelani was a descendant of a noble family from Bologna. He himself designed the sgrafitto murals. This colourful work of art seems purely Italian. The technique was originally Roman. It is a fresco technique, in which the drawing is etched into the plaster and later filled out with paint. It is a cheap but very durable type of decoration that was very popular in Brussels. Sgrafitto murals can be found anywhere in the city, on the houses of the rich and poor alike. The most beautiful Art Nouveau sgrafitto mural is no doubt to be found on the front of Paul Cauchie's house in Rue des Francs in Etterbeek. He was in charge of a design workshop specialising in façade decorations. The entire façade of his house has been coverd in ornamental sgrafitto. The house was built in 1905 in a surprisingly modern Art Nouveau style akin to the Wiener Secession and the work of Mackintosh.

But we have wandered a bit too far afield, for Cauchie's house is too far off Avenue Louise. And we have forgotten to point out Paul Hankar's own home in Rue Defacqz. Alhough it was built in the same year as Horta's first masterpiece it seems more quaint. But it was just as innovative, as a close look at the unique

Around the turn of the century, Brussels had not only considerable creative talent but also excellent craftsmen. The finest proof of this is the monumental stairwell of Hôtel Hannon. In addition, everything is designed and fashioned in a light and playful manner. The many shapes and sizes of wrought-iron work make the stairs appear to float in space. Although this decor appeared modern in 1903, it was not really revolutionary, and certainly not compared with the creations of Horta who redesigned the entire structure of the conventional terraced house.

126

construction of the façade will show. Hankar simply used a different design, inspired by Japanese art.

Early this century Brussels was one big building site. A lot of masterpieces were built before 1910. Because so many architects were active, a confusion of styles emerged. Every single trend in modern architecture was represented. When Cauchie's house was being finished, Joseph Hoffmann built a townhouse for the Stoclet family in the same neighbourhood, which was representative of the austere Viennese Jugendstil.

Two years earlier Hôtel Hannon, an example of French Art Nouveau, was built on the corner of Avenue de la Jonction and Avenue Brugmann. This beautiful house is open to visitors. The government of Wallonia has established its *Centre de la Photographie* here. Edouard Hannon admired Art Nouveau and was an amateur photographer. He had his friend Jules Brunfaut build a Horta-style house. This was unusual, because Brunfaut had only designed straightforward Neo-classical buildings. This house has remained his only Art Nouveau building. Perhaps Hannon helped with the design. Horta's influence is most conspicuous in the imposing stairwell. It is a work of art that unites all of the rooms. The ornamentation is very special. Hannon selected glass windows from Tiffany's and furniture from Emile Gallé. The huge mural in the stairwell is by the French artist Paul-Albert Baudouin. It is very dramatic with its flamboyant characters striding through a colourful landscape. What is striking as well is the deliberate stylistic unity of the ironwork, mosaics and murals. Every last detail was carefully thought out and crafted. Creations like these required great effort. Just think how many hours were required for the design and execution!

We can see from Horta's house and studio how much Horta valued modern industrial materials. Iron constructions are in evidence everywhere, even in the dining room. Up until then, iron had only been used for large buildings such as warehouses or production halls. Other examples include the Eiffel Tower and the greenhouses of Laeken (designed by Horta's mentor Alphonse Balat). However, Horta carefully tempered the industrial nature of the ironwork by giving it an elegant form and colour.

Around the turn of the century, Brussels was in the throes of a new renaissance. Clients with an artistic and social bent were commissioning revolutionary architects to build hyper-modern houses. The clients and architects were strong-willed individuals. An example is the architect Jules Brunfaut, who built a striking residence (above) on the corner of Avenue de la Jonction for Edouard Hannon, an important engineer in the Solvay company. However, Victor Horta was the most innovatory architect of all. For Horta, Art Nouveau was more than just decoration. It was a way of life. In the middle of his house (right), he designed a monumental stairwell with sitting and reception areas. This was the centre of life in the house.

128

The Victor Horta house in rue Américaine is something of a sanctuary. It is rich
in materials but surprisingly simple in its
design lines. The materials used were revolutionary: the balcony above the door, for
example, has a glass floor. The construction is ingenious, and light and fresh air
penetrate the house everywhere. Considerable attention was therefore paid to hygiene.
As much of the furniture has been
preserved, one can still feel the ineffable
presence of Horta. This milestone in
modern architecture has become a museum
to be visited. Visitors can also get some
idea of the intensity of Horta's work.
In addition to drawings, scale models
were made of many of the details.

Above you see the large dining room of the Amadeus. This is a place where visual and culinary pleasures are combined. The painting of the cityscape at the back and to the left is by Agnès Emery. The building betrays its origin as the rough walls and glass canopies are reminders that this was once a workshop where frames were made.

CHRISTIAN NEIRYNCK GRADUATED AS AN architect in the early seventies. At that time architectural colleges were hardly interested in interior design. The consensus was that good architecture did not need decoration. Everyone focused on the architectural divinities of the twentieth century, such as Le Corbusier or the Bauhaus adepts. Earlier architecture was forgotten, a fate that also befell Art Nouveau. At that time a number of masterpieces were torn down, including the Socialist Meeting-Hall, Maison Aubecq and the Blérot home. A great pity. Certainly, there was some opposition, but most people did not realise how outrageous this destruction was. Many modern architects despised the flamboyant romanticism of the *Belle Epoque*. They knew that some representative buildings ought to be preserved, but deep in their hearts they simply thought Art Nouveau was ugly.

Fortunately, there was a change of opinion. Some young designers rediscovered the architecture of Charles Rennie Mackintosh and the Arts and Crafts Movement. They began to resist cold, unimaginative functionalism. Neirynck was one of these newcomers who argued that a home is more than a *machine à vivre*, as Le Corbusier had once claimed. Christian became fascinated by Brussels Art Nouveau and was influenced by it, as his own work shows.

But it took some time for this influence to take effect, for initially he was deeply disappointed by architecture and turned his back on it. He retired to a Buddhist community in the south of France, where he renewed his acquaintance with architecture when the community asked him to design a village. 'That is how my interest was reawakened. It was an unusual challenge, for I had to design something for an entire community,' he says. His friends were highly satisfied with his project and suggested that he should try for the Prix de Rome. Neirynck did and won the award. It was a milestone in his career. But it did not at once set him back on the road to architecture, for he had begun to feel more attracted by interior design.

In 1978 he returned to Belgium, where he tried to find an old factory in the centre of Brussels. At that time no-one thought of converting factories into private homes. He happened to find an empty building with a large house and a workshop attached to it near St Giles, in Rue Veydt off Avenue Louise. It was love at first sight. The building had been used as a frame-making workshop. When Christian walked through the gate it was as if the craftsmen had only just left the building. All the equipment and tools were still there. There were even drawings left on the tables, ready for use. Plaster frame moulds, covered with a layer of dust, were lying about everywhere. Christian soon became aware of the value of his discovery and donated part of the material to the Ixelles museum.

Later the workshop turned out to have been rather special and to have had a chequered past. Before it became a frame-making workshop it had been a printers' shop and before that the rooms had been let to artists. Christian thinks the building must have been a private college of art. One day an elderly lady arrived with an old picture of the college. She said she had posed there as a model. She also claimed that both Fernand Khnopff and Rodin had worked there.

Neirynck was so impressed by his new home that at first he did not know what to do with it. After three months it dawned on him that the building was too large for him and he decided to turn part of it into a restaurant. Meanwhile the Amadeus, as he called his eatery, has become one of the most trendy establishments of Brussels, because of its splendid cuisine and unusual decorations. One of the studios was converted

The building which houses the Amadeus is a jumble of corridors, corners and studios. In a somewhat neglected corner, we discover the library where Christian Neirynck retires to seek inspiration, a dark place full of intimacy. There are few books to be found on architecture: most of them are about painting. Of course, this comes as no surprise as Neirynck designs architectural forms like a painter. He always uses the atmosphere of a house or of a room as the starting-point. He sometimes even feels obliged to preserve the very darkness of a room.

Nowadays, architects' offices are like laboratories, says Christian Neirynck. He cannot understand how people can create in such a sterile environment. In his workshop, you look in vain for any blueprints. There is not even a proper drawing table. The tables are scattered with aquarelles and drawings together with tubes of paint, brushes and charcoal. Each corner of this place is a still-life full of knick-knacks, old odds and ends and tools. Everything here is left to chance, and Neirynck is not the kind of man who restores everything in detail. The interior reflects his adventurous spirit and restless temperament. The above work surface is in the library. At the bottom, we see part of the painter's studio.

The painter's studio is an inner sanctum that must be approached with reverence. The first step into the room is particularly impressive, especially with the northern light that streams in. You are in fact stepping into the history of the building, because the walls are full of different types of mouldings and frames. This was once a frame-making workshop that employed artists, painters and sculptors. In fact, tradition has it that Rodin and Khnopff once worked here. In the middle of the room, there is a méridienne. What an exquisite place for a midday siesta!

into a winter garden. Christian hung a Venetian chandelier there and put a large Neo-classical statue in a room with walls painted in ultramarine. The cocktail bar was painted in dark grey and has been decorated with pieces of old mirrors. Neirynck not only reconceptualised the building's architecture, but he also created its furnishings. Some items, such as the painted townscape and murals were carried out with the help of Agnès Emery. Together they created the pronouncedly Art Nouveau setting of the winebar with its wooden panelling and decorative tiles.

Christian Neirynck lives in an apartment over the Amadeus. His working space consists of three rooms that each have a function of their own. As his studio he uses a room on the north with a huge window through which beautiful light shines in. The walls are covered with plaster frame moulds. Behind an antique screen there is a table with sketchbooks, old compasses and charcoal-filled penholders. The studio offers a splendid view of the méridienne. This is where Neirynck asks his models to pose.

Next door is his study. An old filing cabinet stands against the wall and a wrought-iron chandelier hangs from a ladder. This is not an architect's studio but a curiosity shop. Christian thinks that contemporary architects' offices look like laboratories. He fails to understand how his colleagues can work in such a cold, barren environment.

In the third room, too, with its large drawing table, we look in vain for blueprints. At the back is Christian's library – a modest, rather dark room packed with books. It is like a scriptorium, where the writing materials have been replaced by paint tubes

and brushes. The library does not contain many books about architecture, most volumes deal with painting. No wonder, for Neirynck goes about his job like a painter rather than an architect. For each of his creations he ponders the atmosphere, light and darkness. Chiaroscuro especially is of major importance to him. Unlike many of his colleagues he does not like to open up all the rooms of a house to create vistas that demystify the atmosphere.

Neirynck did not by any means sell his soul to Le Corbusier. He in fact swears by the precursors of the great French architect, Morris and Mackintosh, and he is not a believer in pure functionalism. In his view, good architecture has to be decorative. A house is more than just a machine for dwelling. This can be seen from his own studio. It is in this charming chaos that houses are designed, not as sterile places of residence, but as creations with a real atmosphere in which it is a pleasure to live.

The design features of Agnès Emery's home are surprisingly nonchalant, but her colour palette can still be recognised. The furniture is a hotchpotch of souvenirs. Her mirror room, which is hung from top to bottom with old discarded mirrors, is the one that appeals most to the imagination. This is a feature she has been fascinated with since her childhood, which is hardly surprising since her grandfather made mirrors for a living.

WHEN AGNÈS EMERY WAS YOUNG SHE often visited the Palais Stoclet in Brussels, Josef Hoffmann's masterpiece. It was quite a privilege, for very few people are ever allowed to enter this landmark. Agnès was a friend of one of the children of the family living in the palais. Her grandfather told her to take in as much of the surroundings as she could, because he thought it was a magnificent building. These visits determined the course of her later life. She felt thoroughly charmed by the beauty of this monument to Viennese Art Nouveau. For hours on end she would admire Klimt's murals. Her fascination with Art Nouveau grew stronger and stronger. She and Neirynck were among the first to be inspired by Brussels Art Nouveau.

She owes much to her grandfather. He was an unusual, eccentric man, who would buy Liberty materials to make clothes for his granddaughter. Dressed in them she would pose for his watercolours. It is not surprising that Agnès Emery's work hints at the subdued colour schemes of Liberty designs and William Morris's art. Morris cannot be disregarded when we try to get to the roots of Art Nouveau. Just over a century ago every single architect and designer was fascinated by the furniture, wallpaper and textiles produced by his workshop. Morris has been such a strong influence on Agnès Emery, that she, like him, has set up a workshop. In Noir d'Ivoire, her shop at the foot of Sablon, she exhibits a collection of furniture, textiles and decorative tiles that she designed following the example of masters like Morris, Ruskin and others.

In Agnès's home Morris is permanently present. It is not even necessary to look at her own work. In her studio a large book with furniture paper by Morris hangs from a doorknob. Behind the studio is a library with reference books, including the bible of the Arts and Crafts Movement, *The Grammar of Ornament* by Owen Jones, a richly illustrated book full of strange drawings. This book is now fairly well known thanks to several re-editions, but just a few years ago it was virtually unknown. 'This is the book that inspired the architects,' Agnès Emery says, 'but in my days as a student of architecture I was not even allowed to sneak a glance at it. We were fed on a diet of Modernism, pure shapes only were approved of. Le Corbusier was idolised. All his predecessors were ignored. In fact, we were kept ignorant about art history. Toying about with ornaments was considered a crime. It was forbidden to grace buildings with motifs and colours.'

But forbidden fruit tastes nice. In her grandfather's bookcase she found old volumes of *The Studio*. And in fleamarkets she would look for old books about architecture, cabinetmaking and decoration. In that way she acquired her skills. Ultimately, Agnès Emery never designed a house. She resolutely opted for decorating buildings. For a long time her work was not taken seriously, but now it is. She feels that building involves more than just construction. Decoration and creating an atmosphere are at least as important. She has carried out a good deal of renovations. At first her contributions were limited to creating murals. Now she does many other things as well. She offers total concepts, including tiling floors, decorating walls, and designing curtains and furniture. She has achieved fame with her murals, in which she combines Byzantine and Egyptian motifs with Morris-like patterns. The work is carried out by skilled craftsmen, emulating the practice of the Arts and Crafts Movement.

THE ABUNDANCE OF BRUSSELS ARCHITECture is clear evidence that, from 1890 until the eve of the Great War, the city was exercising a tremendous force of attraction all around Europe. Belgium, a rich and centrally located little country, was very much in vogue among foreigners. Visitors mainly came to the capital and the towns along the coast, and Ostend and Blankenberge were real gems in those days. This international interest also bore artistic fruit, one example being this country house in Uccle. You would never suspect from the plain façade that a renowned architect designed this property. It was built in 1912 under the direction of the French artist and architect Louis Süe. In fact, it is hardly even mentioned in specialised literature and is little known. Süe was not a celebrity before the war. It was only when he founded the Compagnie des Arts Français with André Mare on the corner of the Faubourg Saint-Honoré and

Avenue Matignon that he emerged as one of the great masters of Art Déco. However, there is no trace of all this in this particular house.

Süe designed the property with his then partner, Paul Huillard. You can see from the simple lines that Süe was reacting to the opulence of Art Nouveau, which he disliked. The most appealing room in the house is the dining room on the garden side, gaily appointed with bright ceiling paintings which are the work of Jaulmes, one of the many painters-decorators of mailboats. Süe, Huillard and Jaulmes opted for a style à la Grecque, that is, the Louis XVI style that was then enjoying a brief revival. At that time, Süe was still looking for his own style. This assignment in Brussels was not without historic significance, because we know that at that time he also visited Hoffmann's Palais Stoclet, which certainly influenced him in his great shift towards simple Art Déco.

Around the turn of the century, Brussels was a laboratory where architects came from everywhere to experiment. Just before the outbreak of World War I in 1914, a tremendous amount of building work was still under way, but with somewhat less inspiration than before. Art Nouveau had already for some time been past its heyday, and some architects, like Antoine Pompe, were trying to make this style more austere. Others were endeavouring to define a more purified and functional style. However, some were also flirting with the past. For interiors, the Louis XVI style was coming back into vogue. This monumental dining room is a quite unknown piece of work by the French artist-architect Louis Süe who was one of the great names in Art Déco design during the inter-war period.

Collectors
and Creativity

David van Buuren's house is really a little Dutch island in Brussels. This masterpiece, built from 1924 to 1928, combines the expressionism of the Amsterdam School with Art Déco from Brussels and Paris. On the right, you see the black drawing room with, in the middle, 'The Herdsman' by Gustave van de Woestyne.

ALL CONNOISSEURS AGREE THAT THE FINest tapestries and retables come from Brussels. Art production and collection were flourishing in the city of Bruegel. Members of the nobility and the bourgeoisie alike were collecting innumerable expensive items, but that is an episode from the past. Now history is being rewritten as the city is once again attracting many artists and collectors. Perhaps this is less conspicuous than in Antwerp, where contemporary art appears to be taking root more firmly, although things have to be seen in perspective, because the quantity of modern art that is kept locked away in Brussels homes is quite incredible. Of course, these are private collections that are carefully concealed behind closed doors. Foreign art galleries are well aware of the treasures that Belgian collectors have accumulated. But that is only part of the story. We did not go in search of only the most expensive and rare items. In our view, the ambience and the personality of the collector or artist and his environment are just as fascinating. Anyway, it would be wrong to stick to a strict definition of artist or collector. In fact, the people who steer a middle course between the two are just as fascinating.

Anyone who collects to immerse himself in time and space will certainly have a story to tell. David van Buuren is certainly no exception. He is a descendant of an old Jewish family from Breda in Holland who came and settled in avenue Léo Errera in Uccle. Van Buuren was an irrepressible collector with a fine nose for art and antiques. However, he was something more than the traditional collector of the pre-war period because he enriched the past with the present. This was not by any means easy. Van Buuren, who, I might add, was a banker, would just as readily buy a painting by Pieter Bruegel the Elder as by a more contemporary master. In his large collection you may

come across works by Braque, Ernst, Van Dongen and Van de Woestyne. In addition, he has housed all his collection together in one of the most beautiful pre-war country houses in Brussels. His villa, which can now be visited as a museum, is to Art Déco what the Horta house is to Art Nouveau: a milestone in the history of art. The architecture betrays his Dutch roots, but the furniture is in the pure French tradition. The house also has reminiscences of a more remote past, because one feels here the influence of the young Frank Lloyd Wright.

Van Buuren had two passions in his life: decorating his house and collecting art. To build the house, he called on the services of two unknown architects whom he knew he could mould to his will. He himself evidently decided on the style and decoration. Here and there he even put his hand to designing. The exterior and interior betray very much the influence of the Amsterdam School. However, the inside of the house was in fact decorated by the Parisian Studio Dominique, who have embellished the houses of renowned fashion designers, jewellers and antique dealers. The decorators were given free rein to use lavish amounts of hardwood and supplied the elegant furniture. Van Buuren was not afraid of daring combinations: in the midst of this Art Déco splendour, he has hung his Bruegel and a picturesque landscape by Hercules Seghers; under the drawing room table there is a hyper-modern Mondriaan-style carpet designed by Jaap Gidding, who also worked on the famous Tuschinski Theatre in Amsterdam.

In the hall, you would swear you were in an Amsterdam mansion. There is a monumental chandelier by Jan Eisenloeffel. The stark form of the hall reminds us to some extent of the Palais Stoclet. This is hardly surprising when you remember that Eisenloeffel, like Hoffmann, had Viennese roots.

There is a subdued atmosphere in the study. It was here that Van Buuren had tough negotiations with the art dealers who supplemented his collection. There are several masterpieces to be found here. The writing desk was his favourite piece of furniture. It cost a fortune because it is covered with rare materials, such as shagreen.

The study overlooks the enormous garden, one of the finest in the city. The occupants systematically

The house is richly appointed and embellished with hardwood. In addition to dark rosewood, blonde sycamore wood was used. Van Buuren, who was a banker, ordered his armchairs from the Parisian decorator Dominique, who covered them with Kabyle velvet. The oldest works of art hang in the cosy corner (right). This is where the clash between the modern carpet by Gidding and the paintings by Pieter Bruegel the Elder and Hercules Seghers is at its most daring.

Many different artists worked on the entrance (left) that dates from 1928. The renowned silversmith Jan Eisenloeffel designed the chandelier, while the leaded windows are by designer Jaap Gidding. The statue on the stairs is a creation by George Minne. The stairway is a fine example of Dutch Art Déco.

The dining room (above) is a creation by
decorator Josef Wijnants, a remarkable
ensemble with splendid ceiling lamps in
the style of the Amsterdam School. There
are also wonderful still-life paintings by
Gustave van de Woestyne. On the right,
we find David van Buuren's study. Alice
van Buuren had architect René Pechère
design an enormous garden with a maze
(right).

bought up adjacent plots of land to extend their
pleasure garden. The garden, which was created by
Jules Buyssens and René Pechère, has preserved
much of the spirit of the inter-war period. It even has
a real maze. It is in fact nothing short of amazing that
the property with its excellent collection has remained intact and can now be visited as a museum.
Alice van Buuren, David's wife, played an important
part in this.

The somewhat impoverished district around the Gare du Midi is full of surprises. There, we discovered the workshop that has become the home of Eugénie Collet. She studied art history, went to the famous Vanderkelen school of painting and made a career for herself in films, making decors and looking around for accessories. However, she has added little or nothing to the decor of this old workshop. Everything is intact, its patina – and its history.

THIS IS A HOUSE FULL OF TRAPS, SAID Eugénie Collet waggishly as she let me in, 'It is full of secret cupboards, doors and little nooks and crannies.' She did not in fact have to tell me that as I guessed it as soon as I entered the workshop. Entrance is by way of a large gate. At this point, there is no sign of a house as such, but a sort of storage area piled up with bric-a-brac. There are long ladders against the walls full of dust balls, and which evidently have not been used in living memory. Then you notice a sign on the wall in old-fashioned script: 'Atelier de Peinture Collet' and the mystery is explained. A small stairway leads you to a kind of cellar that is bathed in northern light: surprise! Eugénie then led me to a small structure in the middle of the workshop made of painted wood and lots of glass. It could have been a small summer house from a Scandinavian landscape. However, you are not in the wilds here but in the throbbing heart of the city, only a few hundred yards from the Gare du Midi railway station, a bustling district where life is not as pleasant as it used to be. However, you are nowhere safer than here in this forlorn place. The little glass house was 'the boss's office, that is, my father's and my grandfather's', explains Eugénie. It was always nice and warm here during the winter. The original small stove is still here. Not very long ago this was not a house at all but a real paint workshop. 'When I moved in 12 years ago, I lived upstairs, because my father still worked down here', she adds. Little by little, the workshop became her living quarters and thus she closed a chapter of her family history. 'My great-grandfather set up a paint workshop and a school here at the start of the century', she explains. 'He worked in partnership with the Vanderkelen School. The painters were trained at Vanderkelen and here, six months there for theory

and six months here for practice.' The painter-decorators thus became qualified in the skills of faux marbre, faux bois and *trompe-l'oeil*. All this used to be in big demand in Brussels. Of course, this interest is now resurfacing, because there are now once again many craftsmen like that around. Eugénie herself went to the Vanderkelen school after she studied art history. However, she did not really follow in her forefathers' footsteps. Instead, she made her career in the cinema, building decors and searching for accessories. That explains why the storage area at the entrance is full of odds and ends.

Given her training, of course, she has a passion for decoration. But that is not all. On her mother's side, she has even deeper roots in this discipline. Her great-grandfather was none other than the famous Alban Chambon, one of the most talented decorators of the *Belle Epoque* who, among other things, worked on the Métropole Hotel in Brussels.

At the start of the century, forty craftsman worked in the Atelier Collet. It is now hard to imagine. In the place where Eugénie Collet has installed the kitchen, they used to prepare the paint. This was a real job in itself, because the paint did not come ready-made from the factory as it does now. Many different products were used in this preparation process, and these were kept in the large storage cupboards. Eugénie has preserved the last remaining relics of this old family enterprise in boxes, things like jars of pigments and a handful of brushes. The structure of the property remains intact. Even the inevitable signs of wear, which are in evidence everywhere, have been preserved, and the pulleys that were used to drive the mixing and grinding machines still hang from the ceiling as they did then.

What had been the boss's office has become her drawing room. Nothing appears to have changed,

Here, her own personal history comes to life, as it were, because this paint workshop was founded by her great-grandfather. The cupboards which now contain stacks of tinned food were used by the generations of painters who worked here to store paint, brushes and filling knives. The large drums were used to store pigments. The table on which the vegetables are lying was used to mix the paint. To do this, they used machinery driven by the mechanism that hangs from the ceiling.

and even his little writing desk is still there. But it is certainly not a dull, sedate sitting room. A narrow staircase leads us to the bedroom, an enormous room bathed in northern light, a dream artist's studio. There is in fact a corner where Eugénie draws and paints. The bed is roughly in the middle of the room. Here too, we find a glass house which was once a drying room and is now a bathroom with an antique bathtub. Eugénie Collet cherishes the past. It goes quite a long way back, because she even keeps her correspondence. But she is not really nostalgic. Nonetheless, her ties with her family history are very important to her, so much so that she never wants to move away from here. Yet she does not close herself up in this little world, because she does an amazing amount of travelling.

148

Everything is still there, hardly anything has been touched, not even the boss's office (next page). Eugénie Collet has converted the former drying-room on the first floor into a bathroom. Next to it is her enormous sleeping-room. This is an adventurous home containing a maze of corridors and rooms screened by glass walls. As Eugénie cherishes the past, she has carefully preserved the ensemble. That is exceptional. Moreover, the furnishings are not at all banal.

149

The people who live in this house have a fine nose for curios and have travelled throughout Europe in search of rare objects. But they are rather eclectic. In fact, they prefer religious relics and stuffed animals. This is admittedly a strange, surrealistic combination, but everything somehow goes together. With all this, they have created an artistic amalgam that appeals to the imagination.

Fashion designer and journalist Laurent Dombrowicz and his friend Franck Delmarcelle spend their time on the antiques trail around Europe in search of eccentric treasures. They are particularly pleased when they come across religious relics. The dining room in their house in Avenue du Roi Albert is crammed full of crucifixes, devotional images and stuffed animals. In addition, there is even a gruesome pig's snout over the fireplace surrounded by charming squirrels. There are pheasants and partridges on the wall, and in front of the hearth sleeps a mummified cat retrieved from a quarry.

Franck and Laurent go just about everywhere on the trail of such relics and treasures. They are especially fond of dilapidated buildings. Of course, in this regard they have a soft spot for Brussels, but they find it regrettable that so much is being left to go to seed. It is a pity that splendid mansions from centuries past are left to decay and collapse.

Their passion regularly takes them on a whistle-stop tour of Europe in their van, from Italy to St. Petersburg. Eastern Europe is a real treasure trove. Ten years ago, Prague was a gold mine, but they say that the city has now been plundered and that there is nothing left. Budapest is their base camp, a beautiful city that they say resembles Brussels because the Hungarian capital is also a melting pot of cultures.

Back home, their trouvailles find a place in this simple but comfortable house that dates from around the turn of the century. Although Laurent accompanies Franck on his quests, he is not really the great collector. Of the two, Franck is undoubtedly the decorative brain. On the ground floor of the house, he in fact runs an impressive antiques business. Laurent has many surprising finds to his name, like the Venetian chandeliers in the dining room and the drawing room, the collection of stuffed animals and a small collection of Jasper Ware.

Laurent Dombrowicz and Franck Delmarcelle are no ordinary collectors. They collect what once upon a time was thrown out as old junk. Laurent adds jokingly: 'If they ever offered us Versailles, we would of course be pleased, but we would not be altogether happy. What we really like is good and honest folk art rather than the courtly art of centuries past. Give us any day a rickety farmhouse or a naive painting by an amateur artist. In addition, folk art is anonymous and is seldom signed. They are works of art made by simple country folk with limited means. Anonymity gives this work real charm.'

Their collection contains quite a lot of religious relics made of straw and paper cuttings. There are even little mosaics made of human hair. They are displayed in a decorative but rather sinister fashion behind round glass edged with black frames. These are the fruits of the labours of Parisian barbers who obviously could not bear the thought of throwing away the locks they cut off. Sometimes the hair of dead people was made into an amulet.

In Franck's view, these are precious memories of a bygone era. He in fact spent his youth in a similar interior in the north of France. In contrast, Laurent had a free-thinking education and lived in a modern house full of 'design' features. He finds the old-fashioned world of the imagination both strange and fascinating: 'After I graduated, I began to take an interest in Christian iconography and symbols. It was enchantment at first sight because there are so many exciting aspects to all that. I began to collect devotional art during my time as an undergraduate. In those days you could buy such objects for a song. We were fascinated by these things because they were objects of worship. Each piece was touched and venerated by people, and each piece tells a tale of love and suffering.'

This is a really bizarre decor for a bourgeois house, characterised by a clash of styles that excites one's curiosity. Franck and Laurent have a weakness for funerary art, and there are many cemetery curios among the trouvailles. The two interlocking hands once graced a tombstone and symbolise eternal love.

Through their interest in popular religious art, the two collectors discovered funerary art, an art form that is very rich and emotionally charged. The bedroom is crammed full of such imagery. For example, there is a marble plate with intertwined hands, the hands of a man and a woman who thus pledged eternal love. There is also a plaque hanging on the wall with a winged hour-glass and a small plaque with violets and a setting sun. You can pick up naive art nowadays for next to nothing. Also, a lot of funerary art is now sold at fleamarkets. It is strange to think that sculpted marble is even sold by the kilogramme.

On the second floor, we find ourselves in the theatre decor of the bedrooms. Here, the decoration decidedly has its roots in the French Revolution. The deep blue wall covering with golden lilies (a reference to the coat of arms of the French kings) makes the bedroom dark and mysterious. The two collectors have a love-hate attitude towards the royal dynasty because they are in fact not royalists. However, they certainly have some affinity with the royal family.

Looking around the house, there is evidence of their somewhat roguish approach to collecting. There are symbols everywhere that glamorise the French Revolution and mock the royal dynasty. For example, behind a chandelier there is a Phrygian cap and a drum with the French tricolore. On the bedside table we discover a freemason's necklace. And to add insult to injury, the bedroom is dominated by a heavily sculpted tabernacle from a little chapel in the Auvergne. The decoration of the room is the worse for wear and appears to have been saved just in time from the Revolution.

These two rather original collectors have a passion for time-honoured ornaments, but this cannot be put down to mere nostalgia. They have consciously created a contrast between the decor and the outside world that nowadays is computer-controlled. They find the modern design style meagre, cold and clinical. So would you call this interior old-fashioned? Well, not really, it is actually a style for our times. But it is certainly very different from run-of-the-mill interiors. Here, the occupants of the house have let their sensibility and fantasy run wild. In addition, each objet d'art has its own history. Franck and Laurent consider themselves temporary custodians. This is an extremely interesting way of looking at things. As Laurent points out, 'The most typical feature of old furniture is that it can be adapted to suit the taste of each generation. An old armchair, for example, can be reupholstered or repainted, and this process continues after we are gone. That is really fascinating. In contrast, you cannot do anything with modern furniture. It always looks and is

the same as when it left the factory. As a result, you never become part of the history of the object. In other words, furniture is a key feature of a modern interior. In a house full of antiques, the occupants can alter all the different objects to their own taste. This means that in a modern house you are not quite as free to do what you want. The furniture and the architecture force you to live your life in a certain way. Wherever you go, there are no longer any inherent features that express the local cultural environment.'

The bedroom is, as it were, a tongue-in-cheek tribute to the French royal dynasty. There is a certain amount of humour in the details. Above the tabernacle there is a copper plaque in honour of the French Republic. In a corner of the room, there is a Phrygian cap with a freemason's necklace. With this interior, the collectors have consciously created a contrast with the outside world where everything is computer-controlled.

ARCHITECT LYDIA KÜMEL LIVES IN ONE of the most mysterious houses in Brussels, a deep red painted 'accordion' that sits in splendour on a little hill. With its flat roof and the stark walls full of little square windows, this is a perfect example of functionalism. However, the artwork does not just look mysterious. In effect, the house is in many ways a mystery for art historians because no-one knows for sure who the architect was. One thing we can be sure of is that none of the great names who at that time were working in Brussels, such as Victor Bourgeois, Louis De Koninck, Huib Hoste or Joseph Diongre, could be behind this work. This is rather annoying because the house is strikingly well built. It was constructed around 1927 by the contractor Yvon Beaudoux for a stockbroker. In fact, the contractor himself may (who knows?) have designed the building.

The building came within a hair's breadth of being demolished, a fate from which it was saved by Lydia Kümel. It was in a dreadful state when she found it. There were cats living in the splendid drawing rooms, and many of the windows were bricked up. The sun temple looked more like a forlorn grotto.

With the arrival on the scene of Lydia Kümel, all that changed, and the house was restored to perfection. The monumental entrance with its grand stairway provided a spectacular touch. The symmetrical structure of this artwork and the finishing with black stone and mosaic suggest pure Art Déco. The stairway does not therefore quite fit into the decidedly more modern façade.

By having everything painted white, Lydia has made this house into a perfect constructivistic work of art where the different intersecting geometric forms are an ode to Mondriaan and Doesburg. Truly unforgettable images.

Art dealer Xavier Hufkens commissioned architects Paul Robbrecht, Hilde Daem and José Van Hee to convert an old house into a gallery.
This was no easy task because it was in fact a conventional mansion house. But to free the building from this 'mundanity', much of the neglected interior was replaced by a modern construction that has been appointed with real design virtuosity.

Before the war, Brussels still played a key part in modern architecture, although the city is now overshadowed by Flanders, where architecture is making surprisingly great strides. Many young architects like Stéphane Beel, Philippe Samyn, Eugeen Liebaut, Henk De Smet, Paul Vermeulen, Pascal Van der Kelen and Christian Kieckens are working to raise contemporary architecture to an international level. They are achieving this not only through major projects but also by building modest houses. In the Belgian capital, you have to dig deep to find interesting new constructions. There is a lot of building going on, but the property developers are contenting themselves with inferior creations.

It takes a bit of detective work to find something interesting. Close to the dark, forbidding Porte de Flandre in Molenbeek, there is a bright and airy block of flats designed by the architects Patrick Lootens and Mauro Poponcini from Antwerp. There is also the King Baudouin Stadium by Bob van Reeth and the Natan fashion shop by Vincent Van Duysen. This is only a selection of what is on offer. But the present legacy is not a tremendously rich one, whether you are looking for large buildings or for ordinary houses.

Fortunately, there are some exceptions. The property of art dealer Xavier Hufkens is a truly convincing example of architectural conversion work appointed in the contemporary style. What makes the building all the more fascinating is the tremendous contrast between old and new. Xavier Hufkens entrusted architects Paul Robbrecht, Hilde Daem and José Van Hee with the task of converting this property into an art gallery. This was a very difficult task because the original building was a stately home with a Parisian façade, a charming but terribly bour-

In the middle of the building, on the second floor, the entire construction is split by an enormous oblique shaft (below) that draws light down into the house. This is to be found in the apartment above the gallery. There are works of art everywhere, such as the dated painting by On Kawara (above).

geois construction. The architects managed to preserve some of its original grandeur. One of the drawing rooms has been preserved, and the street side betrays little of the modern approach. However, inside the building, the designers have really pulled out all the stops. The design is quite stark and austere, but very powerful nonetheless. The designers have created spacious rooms that look out over the back garden designed by Jacques Wirtz. The spatial distribution is complex because all the rooms, as it were, flow into each other. In addition, there is also a narrow shaft nine metres high that lets the light in. The exhibition rooms are at the top of the building. One room is referred to as 'upstairs'. Hufkens exhibits in this particular room a number of less well-known artists. The rest of the property is home to works by renowned artists such as Ettore Spalletti, Michelangelo Pistoletto, Yves Oppenheim, Jan Vercruysse and Thierry De Cordier.

In the middle of the building you come across a spacious library which is sedate, modern in form but decidedly old-fashioned in design, because the shelves are very high. Behind the furniture there is a hidden stairway which leads to the living room. There is a smooth transition from the gallery to the living quarters thanks to the gradual evolution of the architecture. A high shaft illuminates the entrance to this deep house. Behind this there are other stairs which lead to the guestrooms upstairs. Some of the rooms were recently decorated by the Antwerp architect's firm of Claire Bataille and Paul Ibens. In Xavier's office a strange, elusive atmosphere is created by the dark wooden panelling, the diffuse light and the furniture by Christian Liaigre.

160

The apartment above the gallery is very solemn in style. It is an interplay of white walls that purify the light. Some of the rooms, such as Xavier Hufkens' study, were recently redesigned. This work was entrusted to the Antwerp-based architect's firm of Claire Bataille and Paul Ibens, who gave it a completely different and somewhat impalpable atmosphere. All the walls are covered with dark wood panelling. One particularly powerful feature in terms of form is the elongated fireplace which makes a huge cut in the wall. Also, a mysterious, diffuse light pervades the room.

The most striking feature is of course the rear façade. This real work of art cannot be seen from the street. It is a refined concrete structure with glass recesses and a fine roof coated with sheet lead that glistens in the sun.

Elvis Pompilio prefers Brussels to Paris. In his view, the Belgian capital is more crazy and exotic and full of surrealistic surprises. He finds it difficult to conceal his weakness for the Fifties. His house is crammed full of bric-a-brac from those crazy days. The vases by Alexandre (above) are the showpieces of his collection.

LESS THAN TEN YEARS AGO, HAT DESIGNER Elvis Pompilio decided to make the move from Liège to Brussels. He says it is a splendid city to live in. 'And I live in the nicest district, close to Manneken Pis. It is still a very popular district that gets visitors of all kinds, young and old people, rich tourists and punks. As far as I am concerned, uptown Brussels is too chic.' He says that Brussels is more fascinating and colourful than respectable Paris where he spends his weekends. The hatter lives next to his shop in a little alley with old buildings. The house was once a milliner's workshop, but he did not know it when he bought it. In what was formerly the showroom, he exhibits his latest creations. He had his workshop converted into an apartment. The living room, the strangest room of all, is surrounded by a mezzanine on which it is impossible to walk around and which used to be a drying area for semi-finished hats. Here Elvis stores stacks of suitcases and boxes.

You could not really call this a sitting room but rather a passageway to the kitchen. Elvis Pompilio explains: 'I tend to spend much more time in the kitchen having a drink with friends. In the evening I seldom spend time in the living room because I can just as easily lie in bed and watch television. Actually, I attach little importance to a living room. For me, it is a storage area, a place to show off different things.' As might be expected, it is full of odds and ends. The most striking features are the three old-fashioned library cabinets full of bizarre vases in faded colours. He explains: 'I started collecting with these vases that were made by a Russian who signed his work Alexandre. Actually, very little is known about him, but his vases can be found everywhere. The oldest date from the 1940s and the most recent from 1962, the year he stopped working. They are so much more amusing and more surrealistic than all the stuff produced during the Thirties. During the Forties and Fifties, designers were daring enough to use abundant bright colours. In addition, Alexandre's vases betray a touch of American optimism, an atmosphere that must have been very much in evidence in Brussels after the war.'

Pompilio has a weakness for the Fifties. In his view, that era was characterised by an uneasy balance between art and kitsch. 'Take one piece in isolation and it is pure kitsch, but in a collection they produce a totally different effect. So the main thing is presentation. Remember that the concept of kitsch is evolving. What used to be junk is now considered valuable. After all, 20 years ago people used to look down on the Thirties. Things can change very fast.'

Cocriamont castle was painstakingly restored. As in years gone by, each room was given its own individual personality. The smoking room on the north side has retained its respectable, bourgeois style. Much of the decoration dates from the era of Napoleon III.

To the south of Brussels you pass through a picturesque landscape speckled with solid Brabant farms built atop rolling hills. The hills alternate with valleys full of bubbling brooks and abundant greenery. Just past Waterloo, in the direction of Charleroi, you come to the ruined Abbey of Villers-la-Ville, undoubtedly one of the most picturesque spots in the district. The solid remains of this Cistercian Abbey are spread throughout a wood. If you follow the path through the ruins, you eventually reach Sart-Dames-Avelines, a small idyllic village with a few houses dotted around the church. If you consult the description of the village dating from 1858, you will see that no houses have been added in the last hundred years. However, something has changed in the valley that runs alongside the church. Nonetheless, it must be said that the event in question took place over a hundred years ago. In 1875, just outside the centre of the village, Hector Lorent built a sizeable country house tucked away behind the trees on the bank of the Dyle. The house was refurbished by Jean-Claude and Anne Rasquinet-de Saint-Georges. Lorent was his great-grandfather, who in turn was bequeathed the property by his great-grand-uncle Gillieaux, who ran a gunpowder factory here. But that was many years ago and the workshops have since become romantic ruins overgrown with greenery. Great-grandfather Lorent transformed the valley into a splendid landscaped estate.

It was here that the master of the house grew up. He has close ties with nature and with the family history. Consequently, he decided to have the house painstakingly restored. This was indeed necessary, because it had been built as a summer house where guests could be received and hunting banquets could be given. The dining rooms were spacious and stylish,

171

'I was brought up in a house where nothing was thrown away. My mother grew up in a castle. There everything was kept until it was threadbare. That is the way I like it,' explains scenery designer Thierry Bosquet. His country house with its complicated groundplan is a picturesque miniature museum.

IT IS NO SECRET THAT SCENERY DESIGNER Thierry Bosquet has nothing in common with Bruegel and has a preference for French elegance above all else. He considers Versailles to be the greatest wonder in the world. Paradoxically, he himself lives in a Bruegelian decor. His country house stands amidst undulating hills and boggy streams full of frogs. Inside, all you hear are birds and cows. This is rural Brabant at its most fertile. To reach his house you have to trudge along rutted roads with cobblestones. However, you first have to run the gauntlet of monotonous suburban districts full of flashy villas and then, in the heart of nature, suddenly you discover behind the tawdriness a real little paradise on earth, a patch of greenery that by some miracle has been spared the onslaught of the property developers. All you find here are some farmhouses, a few little roads and a narrow alley with three little houses. It is in one of these humble dwellings that Bosquet has his pied-à-terre, rather modest, you might say, for someone who spends most of his time in the opera houses of Brussels, New York and St. Petersburg. However, 'appearances deceive' is his motto. As for his house, when you open the front door, you find yourself, as it were, on the stage. This takes some getting used to, because here you do not expect to find any opulence. There is no entrance hall and you walk straight into the dining room. Thierry leaves you no time to catch your breath and leads you to a strange room with a kitchen, study area and tea corner. There is even a grand piano. In the yellow walls there are white recesses cut out for fragments of stucco work. Climbing a steep stairway, you clamber under the roof to the evening drawing room, a real box room with a Venetian chandelier and an Antwerp display cabinet. 'I was brought up in a house where nothing was thrown away,' Thierry says apologetically. 'My mother grew up in a castle. There everything was kept until it was threadbare. That is the way I like it.' Thierry Bosquet is exceedingly fond of objects that bear the marks of the passage of time and trembles at the very idea of drastic renovation. Consequently, he finds it difficult to accept modern Brussels where so much is disappearing. Bosquet laments: 'Brussels became ugly after the 1958 World Fair when people set about demolishing old property everywhere in Europe. Until then, many buildings had been preserved. In fact, the lower part of the city was full of eighteenth-century mansions. In fact, the panelling of my own dining room came from a house that was demolished. I have seen many things disappear.'

However, it should not be thought that he has a loathing for big cities. Nothing could be further from the truth, as he enjoys the hustle and bustle. But he always comes back to this place where no-one can find him. He has lived here for a quarter of a century. At the start, he only occupied the house on the street side. Seven years ago, he bought the rear building as well. The result is a labyrinth of narrow corridors and tiny rooms. There are no large rooms at all. When he moved into the house, he wanted it to be like a monk's cell: 'With white walls and very little furniture. But this did not last very long, because I got bored with the austerity. I began in secret to collect all sorts of things with the idea of doing something with them. One day, I took everything out and just filled this house up.' He now suffers from chronic horror vacui. Not one single wall is safe, and everything is loaded with decoration, from floor to ceiling.

To find the cause of his 'disease' we must go back far into the past. His grandfather was director of the Brussels Théâtre de la Monnaie. 'When I was a child, I had many opportunities to go to the opera,'

he explains, 'I was really fond of it because at that time the opera was very outmoded. It was not at all as fashionable as it is now. Most people found it uninteresting and the theatre-goers were very old. However, it exuded a tremendous charm and the picturesque stage scenery was absolutely adorable. It fascinated me so much that I wanted to become a scenery designer.'

According to Bosquet, a scenery designer has more freedom than an interior decorator, but he must use his wizardry more artfully. He must be able to suggest the most opulent settings with a minimum of resources, and has to content himself with wood, plaster and paint. As for Bosquet's house, you can see everywhere in the interior that he has a real gift for *trompe-l'oeil* painting. He has even painted many of the doors.

The house has certainly been patched up with a gentle hand. 'Everything that was crooked has been preserved,' he explains. 'Just look at the doors and windows. Even when they are replaced, I want them to be crooked. Many people do not understand this. They would want to have big windows here to get a full view of the landscape. They do not appreciate that the charm of this house is precisely that you do not get to see everything. You have to go through the house, and here and there you get a glimpse of the hills.' Bosquet finds imperfection picturesque. This is particularly evident at the rear of the house where many of the floors have subsided. Here the atmosphere of the house comes close to perfection.

The house is a kind of maze. Carefully concealed behind one of the doors is a dark, forbidding room with glass display cabinets. There is hardly any artificial light. Bosquet asks his guests to have a little patience. Then he takes a few small candles from a box, lights them carefully and places them in the cabinets. It seems almost like some kind of Masonic

Between important assignments in Brussels and Paris, Thierry Bosquet builds miniature theatres. He exhibits his creations in a dark backroom where very few people are admitted. They are housed in an old-fashioned wall cabinet behind antique glass. To be able to see them more clearly and admire them, he lights a simple candle inside. The scenery is made of ordinary papier-mâché and little shells picked up on the beach, but these settings conjure up real dream-like images that could never be created on an actual stage. At least not anymore.

175

Once you have negotiated the many narrow corridors and stairways, you finally reach the master's workshop, a quiet corner with a picturesque view of an undulating landscape. Here, too, you find a collection of curios and precious objects. This is the most direct source of inspiration for Bosquet's real stage scenery designs and for the miniature stage settings he creates with seemingly limitless patience. Here we can see how much Bosquet loves to use brushes and paint. All the doors, walls and furniture have been decoratively painted.

ritual. The candlelight reveals that the cabinets contain miniature stage settings. There is a kitchen with pots, pans, dishes and cutlery. A small drawing room seems to have been plucked out of a Venetian palace. Everything is only a few inches tall. Bizarre. The settings look very costly, but Bosquet knocked everything together with nothing but paint, plaster and wood. 'I do this when I am not designing real scenery and have a little more leisure,' he explains. 'And because I cannot sit still, I come here to find distraction.' He is in fact always busy because he spends most of his time looking around for materials.

The display cabinets are slowly filling up. Bosquet's dream is more or less being fulfilled. He once dreamed of becoming the curator of Versailles, but now he has his own palace at home.

In such a small house you would not expect to find opulent decorations. Although Bosquet adapts every detail to his own taste, the house has been carefully renovated. Everything that was crooked has been preserved. Just look at the windows, the many old doors and the subsided floors. The bedroom is tucked away at the back of the house.

Interior designer Dominic Gasparoly travels to get inspiration. This can be seen from all the details of his interior. He likes simplicity, but not tedium. His interior is full of playful notes. In the dining room, he contrasts stark furniture with colourful postcards. In the living room too, you discover sharp contrasts. He dares to use flamboyant materials. One example is the screen with gold leaf. The refined sense of sharp contrast is even in evidence in the furniture he designs, such as the living room table made of wood and stainless steel.

ALMOST TWO CENTURIES AGO, INTERIOR designer Dominic Gasparoly would have had a front seat view of the battle between Napoleon and Wellington. He lives on a hill near Plancenoit, not far from Waterloo, which was the scene in June 1815 of one of the most terrible phases of the fighting. Most of this took place just in front of where he lives, down in the valley he can see from his window.

However, Gasparoly himself would have found himself at loggerheads with both sides because his house looks like the headquarters of American troops. The Stars and Stripes even flutters on the back wall. Gasparoly is not only crazy about the Big Apple. He also worked for some time in the States. You can tell this from the interior that has nothing rustic about it. For him, the landscape is like a drawing framed in the window. From his house the view of the bare hills is very pleasant. Gasparoly is fascinated by the graphic interplay of letters, lines and drawings. That also is American. 'Everywhere you go in New York, you see hoardings that do not disrupt the cityscape but instead reinforce it,' he explains. He has used this feature in his interior. Above the dining table in the kitchen there is a board full of bus tickets, hotel bills, menus and other souvenirs of New York. 'All the stuff you stick in your pockets. When you get home all these things become souvenirs, nice souvenirs that bring back good memories, and the tickets are attractively designed as well,' he says. In the living room there is another board with things he brought back from Rome. 'When I look at them, I travel a little in my mind. It is a really nice way to start the day.'

BEHIND THE ROYAL MUSEUM FOR CENTRAL Africa, the park – with its picturesque fish ponds – is one of the finest in or around Brussels. But it is also a place with a sense of history, because on this site stood the castle of the Counts of Brabant, whose dynasty died out over two centuries ago. Only the chapel and the water mill stand as reminders of the glory that once was. Close to the ducal mill, we discover a modern house that overlooks the ponds. Here, architect Jean-Laurent Périer built a house without ostentation. In his view, a contemporary house does not need any electronic labour-saving devices. Such technical gadgets, he feels, make you forget the essential, the architecture itself.

Périer thought long and hard about his design. He did not want a bland block of concrete with holes for the windows, but a balanced architectural structure that would blend in with the surrounding landscape, in short, a house that would be pleasant to live in. The resulting construction betrays his love of old-fashioned villas. There are wooden floors, ceilings, joists and banisters, all that in one big living space. Périer gave the occupants plenty of freedom of movement. This, of course, is not a feature typical of modern architecture, where every square centimetre has to have a function. Indeed, you are not allowed in most houses to change the position of the paintings or move the furniture. Such constraints create an oppressive feeling. Here, however, there is a lot of room. The long table is big enough to accommodate a sizeable banquet. And everywhere there are walls to exhibit works of art. The house is strikingly appointed with a plethora of antiques and objets d'art. That is also unusual. But that is what life used to be like. Just look at old photographs of modern houses from the Twenties. You will notice African art, figurative paintings and antique furniture, much as you will in this house.

182

The open plan affords the occupants tremendous freedom of movement. The paintings and furniture can be moved easily, and the decoration harmonises perfectly with the design. The house is warmly decorated with objets d'art and antiques. The most fascinating feature is the kitchen with the interior window separating it from the dining room.

Do not look for any modern gadgets in this house, because there are none. In this regard it is old-fashioned, although it is contemporary in structure. Jean-Laurent Périer did not want a monotonous block of concrete and designed a complex structure that blends into the environment.

Craftsmanship and Tradition

Away from the avenues and boulevards, you can discover in the narrow streets of the city many craft workshops. Some of the ateliers work for foreign clients who come looking for wrought-iron work or passementerie or who are in search of a marble artist. In this chapter we lift the veil on the secret address book of interior designers and decorators to reveal places that are totally unknown even to many people who live in the city.

The teachers in the School Van der Kelen have given free rein to their imagination on the wall of the entrance. The most striking feature is the black plinth at the bottom, with 'grand antique' painted on a background of real marble! With brush and palette in hand, the artist puts the finishing touches to a 'sarrancolin'.

IN BRUSSELS, THERE ARE A FEW PLACES WHERE it is well nigh impossible to get in. The most well-known of these is Hoffmann's Palais Stoclet. Perhaps less well known to the man in the street is the Van der Kelen School in St Giles. This is not a museum or a monument, but a school where pupils learn the art of faux bois, faux marbre and *trompe-l'oeil*. The school is highly respected by connoisseurs. It is one of the last institutions in Europe that trains traditional decorative artists. It is a private school that every year takes in only a handful of pupils (who come from just about everywhere). To avoid idle curiosity and unwelcome attention, the teachers keep the press out. The school hardly receives any publicity, but it enjoys a worldwide reputation that reaches places as far away as New York. In addition, its pupils work all around the globe.

The persons who were instrumental in the founding of the school were Pierre Logelain and Alfred Van der Kelen. They both set up a school, the first in 1882 and the second in 1892. The two schools subsequently merged in 1950. The work of the institute has been continued by the family who run the atelier. The course lasts six months and is very intensive. The pupils toil for long hours in the atelier, and they are intensively drilled on the different subjects and have to do hundreds of exercises before they master their trade. They then complete around sixty final works made of marble or wood, including frames and a decor. This is by no means easy, because the standards are very high.

The school is situated in a striking building that dates from 1879 and that was once an ornamental metal workshop. That explains why the façade is richly woven with wrought iron. The Flemish Renaissance-style façade contrasts sharply with the more sober façades in the street.

A stone's throw away from the Palace and the Parliament, where political decision-makers put the finishing touches to polished speeches, a quite different trade is going on as specialised cabinetmakers use their planes, files and polish to restore antique furniture. This workshop is situated in the salons of an eighteenth-century terraced house overlooking the park. Cabinetmakers Denis Taquin and François Carton learned the trade in Paris and are therefore well acquainted with French furniture. Consequently, they tackle the most difficult jobs: the restoration of veneer and marquetry. The workshop itself is tremendously picturesque. The walls are bedecked with tools and old fragments of furniture. This workshop also trains apprentices who then in turn become masters in this fine traditional skill.

IN RUE DUCALE, BETWEEN THE ROYAL PALACE and the Parliament and among the embassies and consulates, there is a workshop that restores fine furniture in an eighteenth-century townhouse built during the Austrian period. This house is home to the atelier of Art-Restauration S.C.R.L. When you enter the building, it is a bit of a squeeze because the corridor is piled high with furniture. On the first floor, you find yourself in a spacious drawing room overlooking the park. This is the workshop. You would in fact expect to find a tastefully appointed middle-class salon here, not a workshop cluttered with dismantled furniture. The walls are bedecked with old tools and fragments of furniture. There is even a box full of bronze fittings. All in all, this workshop would not at all be out of place in the eighteenth century.

François Carton and Denis Taquin's workshop specialises in high-quality furniture with veneer or marquetry. This is the most difficult form of restoration work. While in one corner of the room the underlying wood of an antique writing desk is being restored, in the other corner furniture is being carefully polished with shellac. This is also a difficult job that requires considerable experience. First, the surface is planed and sanded down with a pumice stone, then soaked with lacquer dissolved in methylated spirits. This must be done layer by layer until the desired effect is obtained.

Meanwhile, other craftsmen are hard at work in the other rooms in the building. The Art-Restauration workshop has a large staff, including apprentices who are being broken in to the trade. This takes at least two years as it is a skill that calls for great expertise. Unfortunately, good schools are few and far between. However, we should not really complain in Belgium as a number of schools are working hard to maintain high-quality standards.

FORMERLY, THE FAÇADES OF BRUSSELS concealed countless workshops. Indeed, around the turn of the century there must have been a tremendous number of stucco workshops, decorators, small furniture manufacturers and weavers' workshops. At that time, new residential districts with richly appointed townhouses were popping up in and around all the towns in Belgium. In Brussels all sorts of products were manufactured, including porcelain tiles. After the war, however, many workshops closed down. This was a pity because they had acquired considerable know-how over many generations. Nonetheless, a few managed to keep going. Actually, more survived than one might expect, and when you listen to what is going on among antique dealers and decorators you discover a whole new world. In addition, you find yourself in the most unlikely places, and often in picturesque neighbourhoods. This gives you an alternative way of getting to know the city.

A visit to a workshop is always something of a surprise. A number of workshops are in fact very picturesque and the walls are bedecked with old models. You get to meet craftsmen who have spent years working away on the same piece with the dedication and patience of monks. But these ateliers are certainly not old-fashioned, because you see young people working enthusiastically everywhere you go.

The biggest surprise we got was on Grand Sablon, where the Sunday antiques market is held. A few houses beyond the famous Wittamer patisserie, you come across the antiques shop of Marc-Henri Jaspar Costermans. He runs the Costerman ornamental metal workshop that has been operating for over a century and a half. The workshop produces wrought iron, casts fireplace surrounds and works and finishes copper. The firm has its workshops in a splendid townhouse that dates from the late eighteenth century. The drawing rooms are full of chandeliers made of wrought iron and hammered copper. This atelier where ordinary copper is turned into real works of art is quite unique. From the inner courtyard you can hear the coppersmiths banging on the metal with their specially designed delicate hammers.

It is encouraging to see that young people are still mastering traditional crafts. However, here too, the skills are to a large extent passed on from father to son.

It was the Austrians who two centuries ago brought Italian plasterers to Brussels to decorate ceilings. Less than a century later, the city was once again overwhelmed with ornamental plasterwork when around 1870 every salon in Brussels was enhanced with opulent stucco ornaments. In the words of Baudouin Storme, who with Alain Panier runs the Gesso stucco atelier: 'This was fortunate because it means that there is now a tremendous amount of restoration work to be done'. The workshop was formerly run by Alain's father, Hubert. It was founded in 1925, the year when Art Déco was born, in a series of unused stables behind avenue Louise. Here, where horses used to be kept, young people are now working with antique moulds. The cellar and the attic are crammed full of moulds and bas-reliefs. And in the place where the stable hand had his quarters, there is now a Roman ruin. This collection is, as it were, the memory of the firm. Thanks to this rich collection they are able to restore the most diverse interiors.

A few years ago, there was a bit of a slump in business, but now there is once again plenty of work. The European Community was instrumental in this, as the influx of Eurocrats has meant that average middle-class houses are much sought after again. These are in fact the kinds of houses that are full of ornamental plasterwork. And because of the years of neglect, there are lots of things to be replaced. It is good to see that this dynamic firm is still honouring tradition. The production process has hardly changed, and even the atmosphere of the workshop has been preserved. Stucco restoration work calls for experience, know-how and skill, as sometimes new models have to be moulded in clay. The success of this small firm lies in its made-to-measure approach, so that dimensions and models can easily be adapted.

H ERE, ONE WOULD NOT AT ALL BE SUR-prised to bump into Charles Dickens himself. The great writer, perhaps, may come here on the eve of the Year 2000 to rediscover some of the atmosphere of his own bygone era. However, he would not come here in search of inspiration for *Oliver Twist*. After all, the working conditions that prevail nowadays are a far cry from those of a century ago. In the De Backer workshop, which was founded around a hundred years ago, the industrial revolution is very much alive and well. Indeed, the company even has an original Jacquard weaving machine that is still in working order. 'The oldest machine dates from 1831,' explains with undisguised pride Paul De Backer, who now runs the firm with his wife and his son Benoît. It's a splendid machine that still operates on punch cards. This work of art is half wood, half iron and makes quite a lot of noise. However, this is not at all disturbing. On the contrary, after a while you find the steady hum of the machinery quite pleasant to the ear. In addition, there are spinning wheels and spinning reels to weave the warps which are then used to make the Jacquard. There is even to this day a hand-operated weaving machine. All the machines are beautifully polished and maintained. This should only be expected, as the company is still fully operational. It is in fact one of the last remaining traditional passementerie weaving workshops in Western Europe, and as such, unlike large manufacturing concerns, De Backer is able to handle small specialised jobs. Consequently, there is tremendous demand for restoration work. In a separate workshop, tassels are made in the time-honoured fashion on a small wooden form, and not on a plastic core as is now the case in developing countries. The entire range is on show in the antique display cabinet in the shop.

Here in this workshop, Diderot and d'Alembert would certainly have found plenty of inspiration for their Encyclopédie. It is still possible to go to the workshop of this chair manufacturer and order a crapaud or a marquise. However, you will not find many machines here, as traditional manual production is the order of the day. In addition, all products are made to order, and even the height of the back and the armrests can be tailor-made. Because the work is very labour-intensive, the workshop has a large staff of craftsmen. In the cellar, there are even sculptors who are skilled in producing decorative rocaille work.

The company stands as a testimony to Brussels' long-standing industrial past. At one time, there were many traditional craft workshops in this district of the city between the fleamarket and Sablon. There were printers, book binders, gilders and embroidery workshops and wood turners. All of these are now gone, except for De Backer and de Siffleur in rue des Tanneurs where copper is cast and sold.

Imagine our surprise when close to the Gare du Midi we came across a workshop that manufactures princely chairs. It's as if you were walking into the Encyclopédie of Diderot and d'Alembert. In this traditional workshop, the craftsmen have mastered all the skills of this specialised trade, from woodworking to patina. Furthermore, they work as workshops did in bygone days, using identical methods, applying the same materials and using antique models. The decor is also strikingly picturesque. To complete the atmosphere, Jadot has covered the walls with prints showing extracts of the work of Diderot.

The chair manufacturing business of Vanhamme, named after Jadot's grandfather, was founded around 1870. That was the heyday of the generously padded chair, and the company is therefore very experienced in these skills. Here you can order a crapaud, a marquise or a chaise-longue. All imaginable styles are represented, from decorative Rococo to rigid Classicism. There are also Art Déco models designed for modern interiors. As Lionel Jadot explains, 'The supply is different from what it was. In the days of my grandfather, the choice was limited. He made around 15 models and offered three types of padding material. That was it. Now, however, we have to look around all the time for new models. It's a constant challenge to extend the range. The client has also changed. A few years ago, our clients were exclusively professional decorators, but now we receive orders from more and more individual customers. Apparently traditional craftsmanship is once again appreciated by the public.'

Given the high production and the considerable manual labour involved, there are quite a lot of people working in the workshop. The only machines to be found are in the cellar, and these are used for woodwork. To start with, the wood is sawn into planks. To avoid a lot of wood being lost, templates are used (cardboard profiles that are exactly the same size as each part required). They are also used as models by the sculptors. The sculptors, for their part, are in a separate part of the workshop and use chisels that they have fashioned themselves.

Once all the pieces have been sawn and cut, the piece of furniture is put together with consummate skill in the time-honoured fashion using glue and dozens of clamps. Depending on the style, the new furniture is then painted or French polished. The workshop fashions Gustavian and Biedermeier chairs, and small antique chairs are also restored.

After this finishing work, the chairs go to the upholsterers. There, the cutter, the man who cuts the pieces of material, plies his skills. Before he is involved in the process, the entire chair must be padded. Most of the time, this is done with vegetable crin made of curled coconut fibres and palm leaves. On top of this comes a whole structure made up of layers of fibres and material that is all secured with nails and staples. Finally, a layer of jute is added with coarse cotton on top. Some pieces of furniture involve a lot of needlework to finish off the edges. Amateur upholsterers are unable to make strong and straight edges. In most cases, the chairs are finished by the same upholsterer. The upholsterers all have a wide experience in their craft, and most learned the métier from their father.

Rendezvous

The following places were chosen for their charm or because they are typical of Brussels. The list is certainly not exhaustive, but nevertheless it will give you an opportunity to get to know Brussels better. It is not easy to describe Brussels as a city, so a guide is far from being a superfluous luxury. The lower town contains the historic neighbourhoods and lively residential areas, as well as busy shopping streets like Rue Neuve with its department stores. A little further on, close to the Bourse, we arrive at Rue Antoine Dansaert with its design shops and other trendy spots. Between Grand'Place and the upper town neighbourhoods we find the extremely elegant area around Avenue Louise and Sablon, home to many of the city's antique dealers. Further south are neighbourhoods like Ixelles, St Giles with its Art Nouveau buildings and Uccle, an elegant area with its splendid Avenue Molière.

Eline De Potter

199

HOTELS

RADISSON S.A.S. HOTEL
Rue du Fossé-aux-Loups 47, 1000 Brussels
Tel.: 219 28 28
A leading international hotel with a modern interior design behind an Art Deco façade, which fits in seamlessly in its neighbourhood. The spectacular atrium includes a section of the city's original fortifications. Extremely luxurious. A particularly pleasant place for brunch or a drink.

HOTEL ASTORIA
Rue Royale 103, 1000 Brussels
Tel.: 217 62 90
A luxury hotel from the turn of the century which has lost nothing of its original atmosphere. The spirit of the past lives on in the bedrooms, though the bathrooms have been modernised. The bar is extremely attractive.

HOTEL PALACE
Rue Ginestre 3, 1210 Brussels
Tel.: 203 62 00
This luxury hotel was built in 1910 and is located next to the Botanique arts complex and gardens.
The restoration of the communal areas has proved very successful. The standard rooms are decorated entirely in wood and are truly perfect – unless you would prefer the mythical Grace Kelly suite…. Luxurious.

HOTEL MÉTROPOLE
Place de Brouckère 31, 1000 Brussels
Tel.: 217 23 00
This 19th century luxury hotel has managed to retain its charm. The rooms have been modernised and the third floor still has its own character. Luxurious.

STANHOPE HOTEL
Rue du Commerce 9, 1040 Brussels
Tel.: 506 91 11
A refuge of calm and luxury in an impressive 19th century residence close to the avenue de la Toison d'Or and Boulevard de Waterloo. The interior garden contains suites, and is overlooked from the extremely elegant restaurant. Very busy at lunchtime. Cosy rooms in the English style. Exceptionally luxurious.

HOTEL MANOS STÉPHANIE
Chaussée de Charleroi 28, 1060 Brussels
Tel.: 539 02 50
A 19th century townhouse with crystal chandelier, patina and gold leaf.

Large, comfortable rooms in oak treated with white lead. Courteous service. Affordable luxury.

HOTEL RÉSIDENCE MANOS
Chaussée de Charleroi 100-104,
1060 Brussels
Tel.: 537 96 82
Less expensive and more discreet than the above. All the rooms are different and decorated with antique furniture.

NEW SIRU
Place Rogier 11, 1210 Brussels
Tel.: 217 75 80
This hotel was built in 1910 by the famous architect Antoine Pompe. It has been restored in a stylish and original way – each room has been decorated by an artist in their own personal style. Mid-range prices.

DE BROECK'S HOTEL
Rue Veydt 40, 1050 Brussels
Tel.: 537 40 33
A good address in a large house full of character, close to avenue Louise and the Amadeus restaurant. The rooms have been restored and are exceptionally calm.

LES TOURELLES
Avenue Winston Churchill 135,
1180 Brussels
Tel.: 344 02 84
This hotel is near Place Brugmann in the chic neighbourhoods to the south of Brussels, home to boutiques and antique dealers. It has the old-fashioned charm of a townhouse combined with the relaxed atmosphere of a 'family hotel'.

HOTEL MOZART
Rue du Marché aux Fromages 15A,
1000 Brussels
Tel.: 502 66 61
This exceptionally elegant small hotel, close to Grand'Place, also deserves mention.

HOTEL LLOYD GEORGE
Avenue Lloyd George 12, 1050 Brussels
Tel.: 648 30 72
This small and friendly hotel offers excellent value and is located opposite the Bois de la Cambre park. Its 'Le Café' restaurant is a meeting place for young people from Uccle.

RESTAURANTS

FOR BREAKFAST AND LUNCH

LE PAIN QUOTIDIEN
Sablon area: Grand-Sablon 4,
1000 Brussels
Tel.: 513 51 54. Open daily
Bourse area: Rue Antoine Dansaert 16,
1000 Brussels
Tel.: 502 23 61
Open daily from 7.30 am to 7.30 pm
In the beginning there was one, then
two, and now they are sprouting
everywhere. Large tables have been
placed in tastefully decorated bakeries
where large loaves of leaven bread are
transformed into delicious sandwiches.
The magnificent salads and mouth-
watering patisserie are prepared by
hand, making for a very successful
formula! The restaurant in Rue
Antoine Dansaert remains one of the
most authentic.

WITTAMER
Grand Sablon 12-16, 1000 Brussels
Tel.: 512 37 42
Open daily from 9 am to 6 pm
The firm was started in 1910 and
remains one of the best places for
patisserie and chocolate. The attractive
first-floor dining room offers lunch with
a view of the Sablon square.

LA VACHE QUI REGARDAIT PASSER LE TRAIN
Rue Jean Stas 6, 1060 Brussels
Tel.: 537 37 40
Closed on Sundays and public holidays
Open from 8 am to 7 pm
A fashionable restaurant nestling in the
Avenue Louise neighbourhood with the
atmosphere of a dairy or baker's.
Choose from salads, refined sandwiches
and a huge range of delicious cakes.

LE VIEUX SAINT-MARTIN
Grand Sablon 38, 1000 Brussels
Tel.: 512 64 76
Since 1968 people have been dropping
by here to eat steak tartare and French
fries, drink coffee, read the paper and
keep their finger on the pulse of the
Sablon district.

AUX ARMES DE BRUXELLES
Rue des Bouchers 13, 1000 Brussels
Tel.: 511 55 98
Closed on Mondays
A genuine café-cum-restaurant from
1920 decorated with wood and
metalwork, white tablecloths and cut
flowers. Wonderful cooking featuring
Belgian specialities like tomatoes
stuffed with hand peeled fresh prawns,
lobster 'waterzooi' casserole and stews
made with beer.

CHEZ HENRI
Rue de Flandre 113, 1000 Brussels
Tel.: 219 64 15
This Brussels bistro has tried to keep
the atmosphere of a neighbourhood
restaurant, but prices have increased
considerably. Enjoy the mussels and
French fries, lobster and delicious
oysters.

CHEZ JACQUES
Quai aux Briques 44, 1000 Brussels
Tel.: 513 27 62
Closed on Sundays
One of the few restaurants near Place
Sainte-Catherine, the old fish market,
which has not given in to the
temptation of easy profits from the
passing tourist trade. A small bistro
where fish and shellfish are prepared
in the characteristic Brussels way. A
place where you can find the atmosphere
of Brel's songs, and strongly resistant to
fashions of any kind.

VINCENT
Rue des Dominicains 8-10, 1000 Brussels
Tel.: 511 23 03
Open daily lunchtimes and evenings.
In this area close to Grand'Place,
which is packed with restaurants, the
trick is to find the best. At Vincent
you enter via the busy kitchen and go
into the large dining room decorated
with bucolic and maritime ceramics.
Waiters in white jackets serve all the
classic Belgian dishes including stews,
prawn croquettes, Ostend sole and the
most tender meat. The mood is
friendly – ah, wonderful Brussels!

DE ULTIEME HALLUCINATIE
Rue Royale 316, 1000 Brussels
Tel.: 217 06 14
Closed Saturday lunchtimes and Sundays
Brussels' only Art Nouveau restaurant, located in a fine townhouse built
in 1850, which was saved from the
demolition men by Fred Derich and
his wife before being lovingly restored.
In the rear, in a former winter garden
decorated with rocaille walls, cast-
ironwork and leaded windows with
flower motifs is a lively café-cum-
restaurant, open daily from 11 am to
3 am.

LA MAISON CYGNE
Grand'Place 9, 1000 Brussels
Tel.: 511 82 44
Closed on Saturday lunchtimes and Sundays
This prestigious restaurant, located in a listed building looking out on Grand'Place, stands out in particular for its cuisine and service. Regulars go for lunch to the convivial bar, where some genuine Bruegels are on show.

LA ROUE D'OR
Rue des Chapeliers 26, 1000 Brussels
Tel.: 514 25 54
Open daily from noon to 12.30 midnight
A café and restaurant in the *Belle Epoque* style, with frescos inspired by Magritte. Local specialities.

LA TAVERNE DU PASSAGE
Galerie de la Reine 30, 1000 Brussels
Tel.: 512 37 31/32
Open daily from noon to midnight, except on Wednesdays and Thursdays
An Art Deco café and restaurant in the Galeries St Hubert, where regulars and nightbirds come for a bite to eat after a film or play. The wine cellar has an excellent reputation.

FALSTAFF
Rue Henri Maus 19, 1000 Brussels
Tel.: 511 87 89
Open 24 hours a day, 365 days a year
For years this has been the meeting place par excellence for all kinds of people in the city centre. The main rooms were designed in the 1930s by a pupil of Victor Horta – enjoy the bevelled mirrors, painted ceilings and paste chandeliers. The outside seating area is heated in winter.

LE JARDIN BOTANIQUE
Rue Royale 236, 1000 Brussels
Tel.: 218 83 49
Open daily from 10.30 am to midnight
Located in the pleasing setting of the former greenhouses of the Botanical Gardens, nowadays home to the Cultural Centre of Belgium's French-speaking Community. There is a full menu and daily special every lunchtime. The splendid terrace is open in the summer and overlooks the gardens.

'T KELDERKE
Grand'Place 1, 1000 Brussels
Tel.: 513 73 44
Closed on Mondays, Sundays, public holidays and in June
A genuine bistro in a vaulted 17th century cellar. Excellent for real Brussels cooking: stews made with beer, rabbit in gueuze beer, eel in vegetables, 'stoemp' (a mixture of potatoes and vegetables) and of course mussels and fries.

'T SPINNEKOPKE
Place du Jardin aux Fleurs 1, 1000 Brussels
Tel.: 511 86 95
Closed on Saturday lunchtimes and Sundays
A house built in 1762 decorated with flowers. The decor is redolent of the spirit of old inns: checked tablecloths, wooden panelling and benches. Old posters of local beers decorate the walls. Regulars and students come for the Belgian cuisine and a selection of 100 beers.

COMME CHEZ SOI
Place Rouppe 23, 1000 Brussels
Tel.: 512 29 21
Closed on Sundays and Mondays
One of the gastronomic wonders of Brussels featuring Pierre Wynants as high priest. People come from far and wide as if on pilgrimage to dine here in an atmosphere which refers to Horta.

LA MANUFACTURE
Rue Notre-Dame du Sommeil 12-22, 1000 Brussels
Tel.: 502 25 25
Open noon to 2 pm and 7 to 11 pm
Closed on Saturday lunchtimes and Sundays
This old workshop, formerly used by the Belgian morocco leather worker Delvaux, has been perfectly converted. Now it houses a superb café-cum-restaurant, where in summer you dine under giant bamboo trees. The cuisine hints of the East.

SABLON AREA

AU DUC D'ARENBERG
Petit Sablon 9, 1000 Brussels
Tel.: 511 14 75
Closed on Sundays and public holidays
This fine house dating from 1610 faces Petit Sablon, an elegant 19th century garden lined with bronze statues representing the 16th century guilds. The refined restaurant, where works by the Cobra school are displayed, serves a fine selection of Belgian specialties.

LOLA
Grand Sablon 33, 1000 Brussels
Tel.: 514 24 60
An established fixture in the Sablon area which attracts a busy crowd around its inventive salad bar. Enjoy lunch, served by handsome waiters, in a decor inspired by Mondriaan.

L'ÉCAILLER DU PALAIS ROYAL
Rue Bodenbroeck 18, 1000 Brussels
Tel.: 512 87 51
Closed on Sundays and public holidays
An excellent seafood restaurant where even the seats at the bar are in demand. An excellent cuisine which you never tire of, although it is pricey.

LE WINE BAR
Rue des Pigeons 9, 1000 Brussels
Tel.: 511 44 93
Closed on Sunday lunchtimes
For people tired of the city centre, Le Wine Bar offers a chance to hide away in its 16th-century vaulted cellars near Sablon. Enjoy highly reputed wines by the glass, accompanied by delicious food.

L'IDIOT DU VILLAGE
Rue Notre-Seigneur 2, 1000 Brussels
Tel.: 502 55 82
This former boutique has been decorated with charm and humour, making it a comfortable place where the limited number of tables are much in demand. English china and cutlery for local dishes.

IXELLES AND UCCLE

AU GRAIN DE SEL
Chaussée de Vleurgat 9, 1050 Ixelles
Tel.: 648 18 58
Closed on Sundays and Mondays
An attractive white house near to Place Flagey with Venetian chandeliers. Refined meals at reasonable prices.

DE HOEF
Rue Edith Cavell 218, 1180 Uccle
Tel.: 374 34 17
Closed on Wednesdays
This old inn was attracting visitors back in our great-grand parents' time, when it was a meeting place for artists who would become respectable citizens in the course of time. The rib steak is grilled in the restaurant's fireplace and is certainly worth the detour. Service is courteous, and the deliciously

modest menu offers mouth-watering prawn croquettes, renowned meat dishes and pancakes with caramelised apples – a veritable classic. In warm weather relax out in the shade of the garden.

L'AMADEUS
Rue Veydt 13, 1050 Ixelles
Tel.: 538 34 27
Closed on Mondays
A fine restaurant which is not trapped in tradition, located in a former sculptor's studio in Ixelles where Rodin once worked.
The waitresses in long black aprons, the muted light and the classical music, together with the interior full of bric-a-brac and curios, make this restaurant one of the most magical places in the capital. The glazed spare ribs are one of its specialities and you can also enjoy excellent wines in the adjacent wine bar.

LA BRANCHE D'OLIVIER
Rue d'Angleterre 172, 1180 Uccle
Tel.: 374 47 05
This old local café has undergone the workings of time without losing its village mirrors and bar. Instead, time has turned it into an institution with delicious

fish dishes and market produce. You can easily imagine yourself to be in the countryside.

AU REPOS DE LA MONTAGNE SAINT-JOB
Montagne de Saint-Job 39, 1180 Uccle
Tel.: 375 30 53
This inn, located in a former working-class area in Uccle which has been gentrified by young Uccle families, has followed the evolution of its inhabitants. The restaurant is a place of refuge for its regular customers and city dwellers looking for a village atmosphere. Located on top of a hill, it offers good bistro cuisine including steak tartare, steaks and family dishes served on old wooden tables.

LA QUINCAILLERIE
Rue du Page 45, 1050 Brussels
Tel.: 538 25 53
Closed on Saturday lunchtimes and public holiday lunchtimes
The interior, one of the most striking in Brussels, is a pretext for friendly but expensive cuisine. Nevertheless people keep returning to this former ironmonger's, where the dozens of wooden drawers are a reminder of its previous use. Via the stairs you can

reach the old cabin which was used to keep an eye on the workers.

LE COUVERT D'ARGENT
Place Marie-José 9, 1050 Ixelles
Tel.: 648 45 45
Closed on Sundays and Mondays
Here you find the wonderful cuisine of Stéphane Lengaigne, who learned his art in the grandest restaurants. The slightly over-chic setting is prolonged with an attractive terrace which overlooks the garden. Particularly pleasant in the summer.

LE PAIN ET LE VIN
Chaussée d'Alsemberg 812A, 1180 Uccle
Tel.: 332 22 56
Closed on Sundays
The decor of this Uccle restaurant is sober, but in summer the terrace is very pleasant. On offer is a limited range of excellent products. Eric Bosmann, an illustrious Brussels wine expert, will be pleased to guide you in your choice. Light and refined cuisine.

LE PRÉVOT
Rue Victor Greyson 93, 1050 Ixelles
Tel.: 644 37 78
Closed Saturday lunchtimes, Sundays and public holidays

A charming house which was once a poultry shop and has preserved the original ceramic decor. The cook, who learned his craft from his own love of good food, prepares meals featuring creatively used herbs. Prices are very reasonable. You will feel at home and eat very well.

LES BRASSERIES GEORGES
Avenue Winston Churchill 257, 1180 Uccle
Tel.: 347 21 00. Closed on Sundays
Of all Brussels café-restaurants, Les Brasseries Georges comes closest to a Paris brasserie, although it does not seem open to just anyone. But you are quickly convinced by the ringing cutlery, proper waiters, oyster seller and superb food.

MUSEUMS

THE ROYAL FINE ARTS MUSEUMS

THE MUSEUM OF ANCIENT ART AND 19TH CENTURY ART
Rue de la Régence 3, 1000 Brussels
Tel.: 508 32 11
Open daily from 10 am to noon and from 1 pm to 5 pm
Closed on some public holidays

Large collection of Belgian paintings and fine arts, from the 15th to the 19th century. Superb Flemish primitives, Hieronymous Bosch, Bruegel, Rubens, Van Dyck, Jordaens and others...
An exceptionally rich overview of the main Belgian and foreign schools of painting in the 19th century.

MUSEUM OF MODERN ART
Place Royale 1-2, 1000 Brussels
Tel.: 508 32 11
Open daily from 10 am to 1 pm and from 2 pm to 5 pm
Closed on some public holidays
The museum lies concealed underground and has works by Belgian and foreign artists including major Belgian masters like Permeke, Spilliaert, Wouters, Magritte and Delvaux.

ROYAL MUSEUM OF ART AND HISTORY
Parc du Cinquantenaire 10
Tel.: 741 72 11
Closed on Mondays
These buildings were constructed in the 19th century for the World Fairs of 1888 and 1897. The museum has 140 rooms and shows exhibits from

civilisations all over the world, covering every period from Antiquity to Art Deco. It contains among many other things the reassembled Wolfers jewellery shop designed by Victor Horta.

ROYAL ARMY MUSEUM
Parc du Cinquantenaire 3,
Tel.: 733 44 93
Open daily from 9 am to noon and from 1 pm to 4.45 pm, except on Mondays
Fine collection of swords, fighter aircraft and weapons of every kind. The museum has not really been designed from an educational perspective, but those excited by the art of war will be unable to believe their good fortune. The 130 aircraft, giving an overview of the history of flight, are a genuine must.

AUTOWORLD
Parc du Cinquantenaire
Tel.: 736 52 19
Open daily from 10 am to 6 pm (to 5 pm in winter)
An exceptional collection of over 100 rare cars, superbly displayed in the cast-iron exhibition hall of the Cinquantenaire complex.

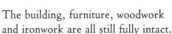

ROYAL MUSEUM FOR CENTRAL AFRICA
Avenue de Tervuren 13, Tervuren
Tel.: 767 54 01
Open daily from 9 am to 5.30 pm, except on Mondays
This surprisingly old-fashioned and somewhat stuffy museum was founded by King Leopold II. The building was designed by Charles Girault, the French architect responsible for the Petit Palais. The Congo, which had been the private property of King Leopold since 1885, came under the control of the Belgian state in 1908. The museum contains one of the world's richest collections of ethnic African art, of which far too little is on display – unfortunately. The fine grounds in the French style offer a very enjoyable stroll.

OTHER MUSEUMS

BELGIAN CENTRE FOR COMIC STRIP ART
Former Waucquez department store
Rue des Sables 20, 1000 Brussels
Tel.: 219 19 80
Open Tuesdays to Sundays from 10 am to 6 pm
In this former department store built

by Victor Horta in the Art Nouveau style you can walk through the history of the strip cartoon in Belgium. The pleasant café-restaurant is a good place for lunch.

THE HANNON HOUSE
Avenue de la Jonction 1, 1050 Brussels
Tel.: 538 42 20
Open Tuesdays to Fridays, from 10 am to 6 pm
This impressive Art Nouveau residence was built for an amateur art photographer, Edouard Hannon. The designer was his friend Jules Brunfaut and the interior is open to visitors. The monumental stairwell is decorated with wall paintings, but unfortunately the Emile Gallé furniture has gone. The house is now home to the Espace photographique Contretype.

THE HORTA MUSEUM
Rue Américaine 25, 1050 Brussels
Tel.: 537 16 92
Open Tuesdays to Sundays from 2 pm to 5.30 pm
This was the workshop and home of the famous architect Victor Horta. It is a perfect example of the Art Nouveau style and even the smallest details were designed by the architect.

The building, furniture, woodwork and ironwork are all still fully intact.

MUSEUM OF FAIRGROUND ORGANS
Rue Walhem 104, 1030 Brussels
Tel.: 241 27 91
Private museum - visitors by appointment
Mr and Mrs Van Gijsel are genuine Bruxellois with a passion for the fairground organs which enlivened many a popular celebration.

IXELLES MUSEUM
Rue Van Volxem 71, 1050 Brussels
Tel.: 511 90 84
Closed on Sundays and Mondays
A small but charming museum in a former slaughterhouse in the heart of a residential neighbourhood. It contains a rich collection of Belgian impressionists and shows particularly interesting temporary exhibitions.

MUSEUM VAN BUUREN
Rue Léo Errera 41, 1180 Uccle
Tel.: 343 48 51
Open on Sundays from 1 to 6 pm and on Mondays from 2 to 6 pm, or by appointment
A superb museum in the Art Deco style from the 1930s, with carpets and furniture by Studio Dominique, Jaap Gidding and Jan Eissenloeffel, and

brilliant collections of paintings from the 15th to the 20th century including works by Bruegel the Elder, Gustave van de Woestijne, Van Dongen, Permeke and Braque. The park is also worth visiting, with its picturesque garden (1924), and the Garden of the Heart, dedicated to a much loved husband. Very charming.

MUSEUM ANTOINE WIERTZ
Rue Vautier 62, 1050 Brussels
Tel.: 648 17 18
Open Tuesdays to Fridays from 10 am to noon and from 1 pm to 5 pm. Also open at weekends every other fortnight.
This museum is a remarkable place, due more to Antoine Wiertz's bombast and extravagance than to his talent. This romantic painter (1806-1865) managed to get the Government to pay for the construction of his villa-cum-workshop in exchange for the bequest to the state of his bombastic canvases, with which he sought to equal Rubens, Raphael and Michelangelo.

GALLERIES

Galerie Xavier Hufkens
Rue Saint-Georges 18, 1050 Brussels
Tel.: 646 63 30
This old townhouse has been converted into contemporary architecture. Xavier Hufkens is a passionate art lover and presents works by Yves Oppenheim, Jan Vercruysse, Spaletti and Pistoletto.

Galerie Meert-Rihoux
Rue du Canal 13, 1000 Brussels
Tel.: 219 14 22
This former warehouse behind the beguinage and not far from the Royal Flemish Theatre is an exhibition space for major figures in contemporary art like Richard Tuttle and Castellani.

Galerie Fred Lanzenberg
Avenue des Klauwaerts 9, 1050 Brussels
Tel.: 647 30 15
This beautiful gallery overlooks the Ixelles ponds and gives both young Belgian artists and established names a chance.

SHOPPING

Centre

Dandoy
Rue au Beurre 31, 1000 Brussels
Tel.: 511 03 26
Open daily until 6.30 pm
For all Belgium's patisserie specialities: Bruges buttons, 'speculoos' biscuits, ginger cake, current bread and Dinant cakes (which are inedible, incidentally, but superb for decoration.)

Elvis Pompilio
Rue du Midi 60, 1000 Brussels
Tel.: 511 11 88
An established designer from the Belgian capital. His leading boutique in the city centre contains hats for every occasion – from caps to wedding veils – for men, women and children. Pompilio is a major figure in the Belgian fashion world and a symbol of imagination and originality.

Galeries St. Hubert
Many dealers in antique jewelry are located in this 19th century covered arcade. Danacqué, in the Galerie des Princes, sells jewels made by the Belgian designers Wouters and Hendrickx.

Here too you will find Neuhaus, the famous chocolate maker, and a shop belonging to Delvaux, the great Belgian leather worker.

Librairie des Galeries
Galerie du Roi 2, 1000 Brussels
Tel.: 511 24 12
Closed on Sundays and Mondays
Since 1941 this bookshop has stocked the most beautiful fine arts and lifestyle books.

Librairie Tropismes
Galerie des Princes 11, 1000 Brussels
Tel.: 512 88 52
Open 1 pm to 6.30 pm on Mondays, 10 am to 6.30 pm on Tuesdays, Wednesdays, Thursdays and Saturdays, from 10 am to 8 pm on Fridays, and from 1.30 to 6.30 pm on Sundays.
One of the most beautiful and best Brussels bookshops, located in a former restaurant with a ceiling painted in the Moorish style.

Mary
Rue Royale 73, 1000 Brussels
Tel.: 217 45 00
Closed on Sundays and Mondays
This Belgian chocolate manufacturer started business in 1919 and is now a purveyor to the Belgian Royal Household. It is among the best in the capital and specialises in dark chocolate.

Posada Art Books
Rue de la Madeleine 29, 1000 Brussels
tel.: 511 08 34
Closed on Sundays and Mondays
Mr Posada has an exceptional selection of books about art and architecture which testify to his own cultural baggage.

Plaizier
Rue des Eperonniers 50, 1000 Brussels
Tel.: 513 47 30
Closed on Sundays and Mondays
If you are looking for postcards without the Manneken Pis statue, then have a look around this shop full of forgotten treasures.

La Boutique de Tintin
Rue de la Colline 19, 1000 Brussels
Tel.: 514 51 52
For everything there is to know about Tintin.

Rue Antoine Dansaert Area

This street is located opposite the stock exchange (the Bourse) near Place Saint-Géry. It is a favourite place for all those in the capital who want to be at the cutting edge in fashion. Some of the boutiques located here are:

Stijl
Rue Antoine Dansaert 74, 1000 Brussels
Tel.: 512 03 13
The temple of Belgian designers in a contemporary decor.

Rue Blanche
Rue Antoine Dansaert 9, 1000 Brussels
Tel.: 512 03 14
This Belgian designer works with fine fabrics.

Sablon-Avenue Louise Area

The Sablon area is full of antique dealers. On Saturdays (9 am to 6 pm) and Sundays (9 am to 2 pm) an antiques and book market is held here. The fleamarket takes place every morning on Place du Jeu de Balle. Here are some highlights:

Philippe Denys - Artus
Rue des Sablons 1, 1000 Brussels
Tel.: 512 36 07
Open daily from 10.30 am to 1 pm and 2.30 pm to 6.30 pm.
Closed on Mondays
In the shadow of the Gothic Church Notre-Dame, Denys sells silver, furniture and art from the turn of the century.

Antiquité Jade
Rue des Minimes 12, 1000 Brussels
Tel.: 512 25 99
Open Tuesday to Saturday from 11.30 am to 6.30 pm, and on Sundays from 11 am to 2.30 pm.
Objects of charm and character from the 18th and 19th centuries.

Costermans
Grand Sablon 5, 1000 Brussels
Tel.: 512 21 33
Open Monday to Friday from 9 am to 6 pm, on Saturdays from 10 am to noon and from 2 pm to 6 pm
For 150 years Costermans have been making decorative items from copper and cast-iron.

Le Pic verre
Rue Ernest Allard 18, 1000 Brussels
Tel.: 513 70 19
Open Tuesdays to Saturdays from 10 am to 6 pm and on Sundays from 10 am to 1 pm
This is THE specialist in antique glass. Here you will find both Venetian glass and crystal from the Val Saint-Lambert factory.

Noir d'Ivoire
Rue de l'Hôpital 25-27, 1000 Brussels
Tel.: 513 58 92
Agnès Emery, an interior decorator who draws inspiration from the Arts and Crafts movement, displays Moroccan earthenware and her own textiles in the William Morris style.

Atmosphères
Rue de Rollebeek 17, 1000 Brussels
Tel.: 513 11 10
Open Tuesdays to Saturdays from 11 am to 6 pm, and on Sundays from 11 am to 2 pm
Discover the charm of Gustave or Provence style furniture, curios, colonial memorabilia and old textiles.

Galerie Yannick David
Rue Watteau 27, 1000 Brussels
Tel.: 513 37 48
Open Tuesdays to Saturdays from 10 am to 6.30 pm, and on Sundays from 11 am to 1 pm
This magical place is like the private museum of a connoisseur, full of furniture and miniature objects from the 17th century to today.

Eric La Pipe
Rue Ernest Allard 9, 1000 Brussels
Tel.: 511 53 24
Paintings from the 18th and 19th centuries.

Gisèle Croës
Boulevard de Waterloo 54, 1000 Brussels
Tel.: 511 82 16
Art from the Far East, China and Japan.

Olivier Strelli
Avenue Louise 72, 1050 Brussels
Tel.: 512 56 07
The master of Belgian prêt-à-porter.

Delvaux
Boulevard de Waterloo 27, 1000 Brussels
Tel.: 513 05 02
This firm has grown from its craft origins and is now based in a splendid townhouse. Delvaux continues to set the tone in high class leather goods: its handbags, suitcases and accessories rival one another in elegance.

MARTINE DOLY
Boulevard de Waterloo 27, 1000 Brussels
Tel.: 512 46 28
'Haute couture' household linen is displayed here with style in a former garage. Enjoy the carefully laid out linen and cotton tablecloths, bed linen, nightshirts, etc.

UCCLE-IXELLES AREA

PARACHUTE JUMP
Chaussée de Waterloo 579,
1060 St Giles
Tel.: 347 49 84
This former pharmacy offers a full range of leisure wear and accessories for men.

FLORISTS

CATLEYA
Avenue Lepoutre 118, 1060 Brussels
Tel.: 344 63 64
Open Tuesdays to Saturdays from 10 am to 8 pm, and until 4 pm on Sundays
The enthusiasm of this young designer gives her shop a marked personal style.

ROUGE PIVOINE
Chaussée de Waterloo 572,
1060 St Giles
Tel.: 347 46 85
Open Mondays to Saturdays from 9 am to 8 pm and on Sundays from 10.30 am to 7 pm
All of Uccle comes to this florist, who was the first to combine flowers and fruit. Specialities include bouquets in a contemporary style and garden and patio accessories.

CAFÉS

LE CIRIO
Rue de la Bourse 18-20, 1000 Brussels
Tel.: 512 13 95
Open daily from 10 am to 1 am
A *belle epoque* café with an old-fashioned, unspoilt atmosphere. People come here to reinvent the world and to enjoy a traditional 'half en half' (white wine and a cocktail of champagne).

LE ROY D'ESPAGNE
Grand'Place 1, 1000 Brussels
Tel.: 513 08 07
A café spread over several floors which strives for the most cheerful atmosphere on Grand'Place. The stuffed horse by the main staircase, the puppets, the

posters and the view of the heart of Brussels make it worth a visit.

LE CERF
Grand'Place 20, 1000 Brussels
Tel.: 511 47 91
Open daily from 11 am to 2 am
A small, elegant and intimate bar where the waiters will be pleased to help you discover the secrets and mood of beautiful Brussels.

LA FLEUR EN PAPIER DORÉ
Rue des Alexiens 55, 1000 Brussels
Tel.: 511 16 59
Open from 11.30 am to 3 am
A café full of history and tales – since its creation it has been a meeting place for artists, particularly for the surrealists in the 1920s, and it still has the special friendly atmosphere of an old city bar.

À LA MORT SUBITE
Rue Montagne aux Herbes Potagères 7, 1000 Brussels
Tel: 513 13 18
Open daily from 10 am to 1 pm
A large, long café which has confirmed its 'real Brussels' reputation with delicious white cheese sandwiches and an excellent selection of beers. Traditional atmosphere.

L'ARCHIDUC
Rue Antoine Dansaert 6, 1000 Brussels
Tel.: 512 06 52
Open daily from 4 pm until late
This café avoids modern fashions and is a place for reflection. The baby grand piano and chamber concerts give it a touch of nostalgia in the 1930s style.

LE THÉÂTRE DE TOONE
Impasse Schuddeveld, 1000 Brussels
Tel.: 511 71 37
A sharp-tongued puppet theatre for adults. Immerse yourself in the authentic atmosphere of Brussels in the theatre's historic café.